Feb 16, 2016

To My Brother Russ. It's an honor to meet you! Thank you! Thank you for your Service - May God Bless!

[signature]

Du Thia, Khoam D., NavyVet, DAV, VFW.

The Escapes and My Journey to Freedom

Du Hua

authorHOUSE®

AuthorHouse™
1663 Liberty Drive
Bloomington, IN 47403
www.authorhouse.com
Phone: 1-800-839-8640

Published by AuthorHouse 8/14/2012

ISBN: 978-1-4772-1061-1 (sc)
ISBN: 978-1-4772-1062-8 (hc)
ISBN: 978-1-4772-1063-5 (e)

Library of Congress Control Number: 2012909380

I

It is dark, very dark, and it is past midnight. I can see almost nothing in front of me, but I have to run, run, run. The Communist police discover us. I have to run for my life. My feet move rapidly as I am leaving the room. My heartbeat is heavy. I run for a short distance, and then I get tripped by a dead limb. I fall hard and smacked my head on the ground. But I have to stand up and run again. I do not want to be killed by the Vietcong police. I do not want to get shot or caught and sent to jail in the deep jungle, where I'd be forced to do hard labor for the Vietcong. The fear is so tremendous that it conquers my pain. I kept telling myself that my life cannot end right here. I will not let the Communists catch me. I need to keep running. It does not matter how dark it is. Even though I can't see anything, my feet keep moving. I run into a big pond full of thick mud and long grass. Oh my God! What is happening to me? I am frightened and out of breath. I am going to be killed by the Vietcong. I am sure that the Communists have me surrounded, with AK-47s pointed at me. I am trembling-- convinced I will die right here in the pond.

That was the flashback of the third time when I tried to flee from the Communists. The escape was once again I'd found myself duped by a deceptive, corrupt organization promising help they never planned to give. In the name of money, many evil men had deceived a lot of people who were desperately trying to escape the country. These groups offered to help people who wanted to flee the Communist regime in exchange for gold and other money and then notified the Communists so the latter could catch and harm the very people they'd promised to help.

I was born in the war zone in the early 1960s in the middle of Vietnam. My great-grandparents came from China and settled in the countryside of Quang Ngai. They'd bought a lot of land for rice fields and were doing very well in this region. At the time I was born, the country was torn apart by the war. Especially in the Quang Ngai province, huge fights constantly broke out between the Vietcong and the Republic of South Vietnam. To a point, this area could no longer be secured. My parents' village had fallen into the hands of the Communists. My family was forced to move a more secure village. My parents lost everything, including their beautiful large home and rice fields. On two bicycles, we had to take what necessities we could. At this time, I was just a very small, four-year-old toddler.

My rough childhood started. Almost every night, I heard the sound of machine guns and explosions. I saw the killing every day. Since my parents had lost everything once they'd moved to the new village, we had to struggle every day. The war had thrown the lives of many poor families off balance. My mother worked very hard so our family could survive.

Then the horror of the 1968 Tet Offensive brought tragedies to the South Vietnamese people. The Communists of North Vietnam deceived the South and launched massive attacks on the day that the people celebrated the most important Vietnamese national holiday—called the Tet Festivities. The armies had agreed to cease-fire during this celebration but the Communists purposely violated. Through these sophisticated and calculated offensives, the Communists intended to gain control and take over the South and they thought they could do that easily. With the national holiday of the New Year, the people and children of the south gathered to celebrate theses special days—to wish that the New Year would bring peace and prosperity to our beautiful country, Vietnam. Instead, the Communists of the north turned the beautiful, spiritual atmosphere into a killing zone. Many innocent men, women, and children were victims. In many cases, entire families were slaughtered because they were caught in the middle of the Communists' sudden attacks.

My village was lucky and did not receive direct attack from the Vietcong. Still, several of my friends and I climbed up on the roofs and watched the fights between the South Vietnamese Air Force helicopters and the Vietcong on the hills. We saw and heard clearly helicopters firing their weapons down the enemies. It was just like a movie, and I remembered it vividly.

The Communists of the North had caused these killings and destructions that imprinted in a small boy's brain. They had no regard for peace or happiness of the normal lives of the innocent people. They took advantage of people, completely unaware, who wanted peace and respected the customs of the whole nation. They had intentionally launched a huge offensive against unarmed civilians without any consideration for human life during the national holiday. It was obvious that these Communists were clearly the worst terrors of our nightmares. They were cold-blooded and possessed evil minds. The regime made every effort to attack and kill the South Vietnamese people without any consideration.

But they failed to realize one thing—the people of the south were brave, much braver than the Vietcong had thought we were. The South Vietnamese armed forces stood up and pushed back these terrible demons and the South Republic defeated the Communists in Tet's Offensive 1968.

After deterring the huge invasion from the north, the people of the south resumed their normal lives; however; the North Vietnamese Communists would never give up their ambition to take over the south. The war went on. My family, like many others, struggled with our day-to-day lives.

I was old enough so my father was able to enroll me in a local school. I was so happy because I was always eager to learn and play. I had a lot of good times with my friends. We made toys together, using soda cans to make toy vehicles and bamboo sticks to make guns. Many nights, we had much fun together under the moonlight.

Suddenly one night, while we were playing, an unfamiliar noise erupted in the middle of the playground. The rat-a-tat-tat of machine guns had totally erased the peaceful atmosphere and turned it into a night of horror.

"Let's run!" my friends shouted.

The shooting continued for next several minutes long. I ran home quickly, and my whole family rushed into a bunker inside our home. I realized that the Vietcong had launched an attack on our village. The horror night was over, but consequently, much tragic news spread through the village the next morning. One of the horrible pieces of news was that my best friend's father had been shot and killed in the night.

Seeing my friend and his family standing around his father's body weeping was terribly painful. Why did this have to happen? I was just a small boy, but I was so upset. A thick cloud of sorrow had covered the brightness of the moonlight and turned the whole village to a place of mourning for my friend's father. He was a good, innocent man. Why had the Vietcong taken his life? Why had my friend lost his father? I had no answer. At this time, I was just a little boy, but I had learned so much about the Communists.

Life moved on, and I continued to go school with my friend. I got closer to him and often comforted him or cried with him when he missed his father. Then another horrible event happened. One night, another friend's family of mine was attacked by the Vietcong. They launched a B-40 missile directly into the bedroom where the father and three sons were sleeping. All four were killed; only the mother, who was sleeping in a different room, survived. Again, tragic news hit the entire village! The Vietcong had murdered my friend and his father. I went and saw the bloody scene with all the bodies lying on the floor. It was so sorrowful. The killings brought so much anguish to the people of my village. As a child, my mind was tormented. Why did the Vietcong keep brutalizing my people?

Time went by, and I started my high school year. The war continued worsening and spreading out everywhere in the country. Worries and insecurities were constantly on people's minds. We could not live in peace. One day, the nightmarish scenes arrived at my village. I noticed that a lot of people, including my friends, were running to the side of the Tra Khuc River. I followed my friends and looked into the river. Two huge human bodies floated downstream. I was shocked and scared I told myself, "*this is what the Vietcong do.*" The regime was totally inhumane, heartless, and evil. I felt so sad and I couldn't contain my emotion. I thought that one of those bodies could be my brother, and tears filled my eyes. All of the villagers believed that those huge bodies were American bodies. I wondered what had happened to them and how they had been killed. My heart went out to their souls and to their families, and I prayed that they went to Heaven with God.

I continued to hear more and more gunshots and explosions every night. At times we had to get into the bunker because of loud explosions and the sounds of machine guns. Families in the village received bad news regularly—someone's father was killed, someone's brother was injured in combat—every day. Many of the fathers and brothers belonged to the Army of the Republic of Vietnam. My parents had their own son and a son-in-law in the armed forces. These were the people who stood up, defended, and protected the freedom and democracy of the people of South Vietnam. I always admired and respected them. Several of my friends and I got together and made a kids' band. We sang many songs to praise the soldiers who were on the front lines and made the ultimate sacrifices for their families and their country. They were my heroes. As a young boy,

I dreamed of becoming a soldier to fight the Communists and protect freedom of my country.

The war grew larger and larger. Its intensity had reached the climax. One time, the Vietcong were trying to blow up the main long bridge of the Tra Khuc River. The Communists employed divers who dove beneath the surface in an attempt to get to the foot of the bridge with hundreds of pounds of dynamite in the middle of the night. Fortunately, the evil deed of the Vietcong was detected and stopped by brilliant South Vietnamese soldiers. Other times, I even saw with my own eyes that military jets dropping bombs in the battlefield which was not too far from where my village was.

One day, my parents received bad news about my brother. He had been injured in combat. My mother cried for days and nights, praying for his safety. After he was wounded, my brother was transported to one of the military hospitals. My mother took me with her to see my brother in the hospital. I was so happy to see him alive. Big bandage covered the wound on his leg, but he was okay.

Then I looked around. I saw so many wounded soldiers. Many were missing appendages. What a devastating scene! There were no words to describe my grief. My mother grabbed my brother and pulled him into her arms. She put her head on my brother's chest and cried hysterically. She was thankful to God that my

My brother, a soldier of Artillery Unit, South Vietnamese Army.

brother was still there for her. I closed my eyes. I tried to absorb all the pain of a mother, who had just seen her son got wounded from a combat. It was just too much to take. After a few hours with my brother, we had to leave. I said good-bye to my brother and told him I loved him. I also told myself one day that I would become a soldier and join him on the front lines.

The war grew more intense. The summer of 1972 was heated to the maximum scale, with large battles on both sides, and consequently, many casualties. The mountains were no longer green; the flowers no longer bloomed; the sky was no longer blue with all the bombings, fighting, explosions, and destruction. The mothers and wives at home received tragic news; their sons, their husbands would never come back home again. Day after day, people lived in fear and misery. Northern Communists had determined to invade the south, and it seemed like nothing could stop the worst evil of mankind. The people all over the south endured so much suffering. Killings and destructions had become everyday life everywhere in my beloved country.

Perhaps signs emerged that the Republic of Vietnam didn't have enough strength to defend the country. The South Vietnamese Army grew weaker and lost many posts. Then, city-by-city, South Vietnam was defeated. Consequently, the Communists started launching a large attack on the Quang Ngai province. Oh my God! What chaos it was. I was just a little boy, but I remembered clearly the nightmare of the night before the fall of Quang Ngai.

Everybody knew that the Vietcong would be here soon to occupy the region and everyone had to get out of Quang Ngai. En masse, people tried to reach Da Nang, the city that was still occupied by the South Vietnamese Army. It was a hundreds miles away, but millions walked on the only road—Quoc Lo So. 1—toward Da Nang. Everyone's state of mind was in intense; people worried and cried out; no one wanted to leave their homes and their village. My family, just like many others, was getting ready to head out and moved north to Da Nang. My father, brother, and sisters were trying to stack all the food and necessary belongings on the two bikes that we owned. We tied our belongings up, but things kept falling down because there wasn't enough room for the things my mother wanted to take with us. Finally, we did what we could, and then we headed to the street.

We saw hell in front of us. No words could describe one of the scariest situations anyone could witness. As the day fell into evening, the street filled with men, women, and children, along with their vehicles and belongings, mixing with military personnel and transportation. Constantly, we heard people and children screaming, crying, and shooting. This was the most compact, disordered large group of people anyone could imagine.

"*I am so scared!*" I shouted to my mother. I held my mother's hand tightly as we walked.

Suddenly we heard a big explosion, followed by loud screaming and crying only a short distance away.

"*Stop walking!*" my mother shouted.

My father looked at her. "*What are we going to do?*" he asked.

My mother did not answer, but she pulled my sisters and brother and me together, and then she burst into tears, sobbing silently. Then we all cried in the middle of the ocean of people. My mother told my father that we needed to go back home; otherwise, we would all be killed on the street. We would rather die at home than on the street of hell. The chaos was unfathomable.

After traveling less than a kilometer from the village, we turned around and went back home. We unloaded our things from the bicycles, and then we held each other and cried. My mother started talking about my brother. He was still in the South Vietnamese Army and she was cried for his safety. He was probably fighting with the Vietcong in some battle, and he probably got killed.

My mother also thought of my sister and her family, who lived in the south; this part of the country still belonged to the Republic of South Vietnam. We were now separated by two different worlds, and we thought we would never see each other again.

The Communist regime had insisted on invading the south. The regime had ruined and devastated the entire population of the South Vietnamese people. Violence, killings, and suffering consumed all over my motherland.

We met some villagers who had gone far away from the village but had been forced to return, and they told us horrible stories. They even told us that tanks were running over human bodies.

Time slowly passed, and we were all anxious to see what would happen. The next morning, my family woke up after a night of exhaustion and we heard so much noise of rolling sound coming from the main street. Together with my several friends, I ran quickly to the street. Oh my Lord! I could not believe what I saw. A line of big tanks rumbled through the middle of the street, and lines of Communist soldiers armed with AK-47s stood on both sides of the road. They were in position, ready to kill, kill, and kill. I was paralyzed with fear.

It was official—Quang Ngai city had completely fallen into the hands of the Communists. My parents still had no contact with my brother or my sister. The atmosphere was very strange to everyone. It was springtime, but we saw no flower blossoms or young, green leaves on the trees; however, we all smelled fear and death. Time after time, we heard dreadful news from the villagers. The family of one of my friends in the village had committed suicide. The father had killed all three sons and his wife. The father was in the South Vietnamese Army, and his family had opted to die rather than live with the Communists. Also, we heard that the local Vietcong had taken several men of the village away. Whenever this happened, those men would never return home to their families. Now the regime had utter control. The Vietcong could arrest, brutalize or kill whomever they wanted.

Day after day went slowly by; then came worse news for the entire Republic of South Vietnam—the Fall of Saigon in April 1975. This was it. The entire government of South Vietnam had collapsed. I was still a little boy but I became upset. How could the bravery of the South Vietnamese Army be defeated? I remembered how my friends and I had sung and praised the courage of our armed forces—the heroics of these marines, sailors, air force, and soldiers of South Vietnam. I had dreamed of becoming one when I was just a small boy. What had happened? The thick, dark cloud had covered the entire beautiful my country of Vietnam.

After that very sad news, my parents started to look for my brother, hoping he was still alive. They also tried to contact my sister and her family. Thank God my parents got news from them. My brother was still alive, and somehow, he'd managed to go to live with my sister in the south after his army unit was overtaken by the enemy.

As soon as my mother could, she went to Vung Tau where they lived and met with them. After seeing them, my mother said that my brother wanted to go with her to Quang Ngai so he could live by his parents, but my mother did not let him. She knew that the local Vietcong would kill him as soon as they saw him. These Vietcong had the reputation of being brutal, inhumane, and cold-blooded. My mother told my brother he would be better off staying with my sister's family and trying to make a living there. He listened and did what my mother told him to do.

When my mother returned to Quang Ngai, my parents now faced the task of figuring out how the family would survive under the frightful circumstances. My mother was a good businesswoman. She was able to build a small business so we all could survive one day at a time. I walked for many kilometers to the marketplace to bring lunch for my mother while she was busy working. She worked so hard for us. Then things changed. The local communists forced everyone to go to the countryside to make a living in agriculture. My parents had to move our family to the original village where my grandparents had once lived with the huge houses and rice fields.

As a young boy, I was always interested in learning about my ancestors' lands. I asked my parents whether the house of my grandparents would still be there, along with the beautiful garden and rice fields. They sadly said no because they knew the area had been bombed heavily during the war. Nevertheless, I was still eager to go back and see my grandfather's land.

Then one day it happened. We arrived at my grandparents' land. My father pointed at one area and told me that the huge house had been on this location. But now this area was all jungle, and several fifty-foot holes made by B-52-bombs splintered the area. My parents could barely recognize the surroundings after having left the village more than ten years earlier. What had once been a beautiful, civilized, village with my grandparents' magnificent home was now the wild jungle with big holes in the ground. We were heartbroken. What did we have to do now? The war had destroyed my father's home and my fatherland. It had caused so much suffering. We had to start all over again from nothing. But how could we do this? My father was old.

Fortunately, I had a second brother, who was full of energy, and he was ready to take the responsibilities for the household and help my parents. First, my brother had to build the shelter. We did not have much of the building materials. We reused and savaged some old materials from the previous home, but what remained was not enough for anything. We had to take trees down and use the wood for shelter.

My brother had built a shed to shelter the family in the middle of the jungle at last. Next, we had to uncover the wild land and turn it into a field of vegetables and potatoes. I was just a thirteen-years-old boy, but by watching my second brother working very hard and my mother struggling to do business at the local market, I wanted to help out. I got up very early in the morning and worked with my brother until late at night. I helped him build our tiny house. I went along with him to clear the wild land so we could turn it into fields of vegetables and potatoes. We worked our fingers to the bone. On many days, I became utterly exhausted and drained because I had worked so hard and had not had enough good nutritional food intakes. I was just a young teenager, and this was the age for growth, but I was only getting skinnier. On many occasions I became very ill, but no medical doctors or nurses or any medicine were available.

One time, I had a serious, high fever, but my mother only took different leaves from different trees. She fried them to charcoal, and then she made me take it. I really did not think that helped me at all but it only made me sicker. But somehow, someway, I overcame my illness. Maybe God did not want me to die yet. I had to survive. I needed to see the life under the Vietnamese Communist brutal regime.

The days of struggle continued. We ran out of firewood for cooking, and my mother asked me to go to the deep mountains to look for dry wood. The mountains were about twenty to thirty kilometers away. I got up very early in the morning around four o'clock and went together with a few friends to the mountains. We carried with us some food and water and a heavy-duty woodcutting knife. We walked for a few hours, and by the time we reached the mountains; the sun had started to rise. We began looking for firewood. It was so hard for me. I could hardly see any firewood, but my friends were so good. They knew what to do and collected the firewood much more quickly than I did. After we thought we had enough, we needed to tie the firewood together nicely so we could carry them home. I had a harder time putting everything together, so my friends helped me.

After having lunch, we began the most difficult process, which was carrying the firewood home. I put two bundles of firewood on my shoulder and started walking. The firewood seemed light enough on my shoulder when I walked the first few hundred meters, but then the bundles got heavier and heavier with every extra step I took. The sun was up high, and the heat was intense. Oh my God! I still had long kilometers to walk. My shoulders began to ache and my energy was running out. I started taking break after break, but my body got so weak I could hardly move anymore. I became extremely thirsty, and I had no more water. I looked around, and I could see no clean water anywhere, but my mouth totally dry and it desperately needed water. Down in front of me was a tiny, shallow pond, but the water was a yellowish color. I didn't care, I put my head down and put my mouth on the surface of this shallow pond and drank the contaminated water anyway.

I started talking to myself. *"Mom and Dad, I am suffering too much, and I am dying!"*

I was determined to take the firewood home so my sister could cook food for my parents. I kept dragging these two bundles of wood, and I eventually arrived home. I became very sick the next two days.

One day, my parents got the order from the local Vietcong—every new family in the village had to follow the Vietcong leaders to the rice fields that had been abandoned for over ten of years. The Vietcong then assigned the fields, section by section, to the new villagers. The regime assigned bad sections to the people who had connections to the former government; our family was among those. Even though my ancestors had owned the largest, best rice field on this land years ago, we had no authority over the land now. Most of the good land here should have belonged to our family but now they belonged to the local Vietcong. They had taken everything away from us and now they gave my mother two bad pieces of rice field. The Vietcong told us that we had to convert these wild lands into the fields of rice by our own hands and fingers. Our survival would depend on that. My parents just had to do whatever they were asked. That way they wouldn't pick on our family.

Tremendous amounts of work were ahead of us. We had to show the Vietcong that we would work very hard. The Vietcong wanted to see us really suffer. That would make them happy. At the same time, we didn't want to provoke them in anyway. After my parents were assigned that rice field, my brother, sisters, and I worked long hours. We used different kinds of shovels to clear those wild bushes and tall grass on the field. The land was also very muddy and we had to do everything by hand. We worked under the rain, in the extreme heat, or under any condition. It was a living hell. My brother and I got burned out and exhausted every day, but we had to do it. We had to make believe we were happy and eager to live under the Communist rule.

Day after day, my mother worked in a distant market so she could make some money to buy food. One day, I had to ride a bike to the market to see my mother. She bought some household supplies and a big bag of rice for me to take home. Late in the afternoon, I tied up everything on my bike and headed home, which was about three hours away. I rode the bike for an hour until the bad road caused me to fall. I tried to get the bike up, but it was too heavy because of the bag of rice. I exerted all my strength and finally kept the bike standing up. I kept riding for a short distance, and then I fell again. The road was so bad; a thick layer of dust covered an uneven layer of rock. Once again, I tried to push my bike back up and continue to ride; but my bike kept falling and falling. It had gotten dark now and I could no longer see the road. I stood my bike up, but I did not know what to do. I burst into tears, thinking that my brother and sisters waited for me to take the rice home so they could cook the evening meal.

Suddenly, a man, who looked younger than my father, asked me what happened. In tears, I told him that I needed to take this bag of rice to my brother and sisters. He told me my destination was still a good distance away and pointed out that I would not see the road at nighttime. He asked me to stay the night in his home and get back to the road in the morning. I listened to him and appreciated him very much for helping me and letting me stay in his home for the night. He helped me get the bike to his home. He also gave me some food for the evening and showed me the bed that I would rest in. That man was my angel. God sent him to give me a helping hand.

I got up in the morning and I couldn't thank him enough. He told me that there was still a small section of bad road ahead. He asked me not to ride but to walk with the bike until I could see that the better road. I did what he taught me, and I finally arrived home that morning.

Life went on. We all worked very hard so our family could survive. At fourteen years of age, I continued to work and help my parents. But there was something missing; my parents mentioned my education. They wanted me to be in school. Since the Communists had taken over, I hadn't been to school. My old high school had been destroyed because that school was funded by the South Vietnamese Army. Now the local Communists had just built a high school in the new village. My parents tried to enroll me, but I was not allowed because of the black mark of my family background.

However, the local Vietcong did reveal that, in order to remove the black mark in my family background, my brother must join the Communist army. I was still a young boy, and I was not sure of my parents' plan. Then the shock rippled through my body. My second brother enrolled in the Communist army.

It was a very sad moment for me when my brother told me what he had done. He was the man of the house, and if he was gone, how would my family live? Moreover, the Communists had always been family's opponents. But, he told me, *"Don't you worry. I do this for our family and for you. I want the Vietcong to let us loose and not pick on our family so that our lives will be easier when we live with them. I will be back home in a few years, and hopefully, you will be allowed to get some education."*

Then the day arrived—the day my second brother had to leave the nest and join the Communists' armed forces. It was one of my saddest days. Seeing him packed his bag and leave our house was utterly painful. Tears filled my eyes as I watched him walk away until he had disappeared in the crowd. I knew things would get tougher for my family. My entire family would be struggling much more without him, and I would miss him desperately.

Time passed slowly. After my brother left, our family turned to a new chapter. I stepped up and took more responsibilities. I worked even harder to take care of the potatoes and vegetable gardens and the rice fields.

One good thing had happened to me. My mother took me back to the school and she was able to enroll me for the next school year. The Vietcong had finally allowed me to register because my brother was now in the Communist army. I was very happy to go back to school, but I also thought of my brother often. I still remember very well the first day I went back to school. I was so excited with new clothes, notebooks, and pens as I walked to school. I also made lot of friends. The majority of my friends in the village school were former Vietcong guerillas as very young teenagers. They were children, and they had been the sharp weapons for the Communists; these children were easily and totally brainwashed by their Vietcong leaders. They fought for the Communists to their nails against the South Vietnamese and the American soldiers. They told me many incredible stories; they were just children, but they had taken many human lives. I just couldn't believe the sad reality—that the Communists had purposely trained children to become real killing war soldiers.

II

$\mathcal{I}$concentrated and focused in school. I wanted to do well, and I did really well for the most part. I loved math, science, chemistry, and physics. I was always either ranked first or second in my class. I, sometimes, represented the school and competed with other schools at math competitions that involved in the entire city. And at times, I won trophies for our school. I wrote letters to my brother, and he was very happy, thrilled, and proud.

On the other hand, I did not do so well on one part of the school's curriculum—the political section which students should praise Uncle Ho Chi Minh and his Communist party.

Troubling news had come to me one time. As students under the Communist regime, we had to do whatever the school administrators asked us to do. That time, they ordered my entire class to walk four hours while pulling a big wagon to a location to deliver office furniture for their leaders to use. My classmates and I were being punished. We were all exhausted from pulling the wagon full of furniture on a bad road for a very long distance in the extreme heat of a sunny day. That was a horrible, unbelievable task for children this age. But that was not all. A few months later, we were asked to do the same assignment again. I got very upset and disagreed with the leaders of the school. I spoke with several friends, and suddenly, we all spoke loudly and expressed our disagreement to our school. We were just students and we were just young kids; we should not be punished in such way.

I was in trouble the next day. The chairman of the school suspended me from school until further notice. The administration called my mother, asking her to go to the school office so they could have a long talk with her. They accused me of starting a movement to against the school and the Communist party. I was very sad to have caused trouble for my family. I didn't know what to do. I stayed home for a few weeks until my mother went back to the school office and insisted that her son hadn't meant to start a movement against the local Vietcong. They finally listened and called me back to school; they were convinced, in part because they didn't want to lose their best student, who had often represented their school.

I was very happy to return to school, and I promised my mother that I would not cause her trouble again. I always wanted to be a good son and did my best to reduce my parents' stress and worries. I studied hard and did well in school.

I also grew vegetables and greens in the gardens after school. Many times I knew that we were low in food, such as rice and potatoes, in the household. I went with my friends to the harvesting rice fields and collected any rice that was left over. I would collect for an entire day for just about half a kilogram. The same thing went for collecting potatoes. I would walk for a long distance, carrying a shovel, and look for the harvesting field of potatoes. I would dig deep in the ground in search of the potatoes the previous collectors had missed.

Attending the Communists school was tough. Students were assigned big, hard-labor projects every few months. One time, our whole class had to participate in digging a man-made irrigation canal, which was several hundred kilometers long and led from the highland to the rice fields. Students worked from dawn to dusk for several days straight. We used shovels to dig, put dirt in baskets, and carried the baskets to a location where we unloaded the dirt to make the big and long canal. Several months later, we were told that the project had failed; it had been abandoned and the canal had been left half dry. What a waste! Didn't they know how much time, energy, and effort the young teenagers had poured into this? I knew that they didn't care.

Life got increasingly more difficult. My parents also worried about my first brother and my sister's family living in the south. Then my parents received a letter from my sister. My sister asked my mother to come and visit her family, saying she needed to see my mother immediately. We were frightened of the news. My mother had to get time off from her business and arrange for the long trip to the south, Vung Tau city. Before leaving, she needed to make sure we would all survive while she was away.

After a few weeks, my mother returned. She broke big news to the family. We were shocked; none of us would ever have imagined what she told us. My first brother, who was a soldier for the Republic of South Vietnam, had escaped the country and made it safely to a free land; he now lived in the United States of America.

At this time, I was about sixteen years old. I had a hard time comprehending what my mother was telling us. How could my brother possibly do that? We lived so far away in the countryside with the local Vietcong and we had no means of getting news from the rest of the country—no radio or television. Even when we received letters from family members, the local Vietcong would open and read those letters before we got to read them. So when we wrote letters, we had to be extremely careful.

The local Vietcong here had total control of the entire population in my village. However, in the South, especially in larger cities, the concentrated population made it more difficult for the Vietcong to take control. People who lived in the South were more aware of the trends of any revolution within the country. After the Fall of Saigon, the South Vietnamese tried to flee from the brutal Communists, especially individuals and families who formerly belonged to the South Vietnamese government.

The waves of people fleeing from Vietnam started in 1976. Two ways to escape the Communists of Vietnam were by foot or by boat. To escape by foot, one had to go up to the highland of jungle through Cambodia, Laos and then to Thailand. The journey would take a few weeks to a few months of walking, and it would be extremely difficult and complicated. The majority people who attempted to escape this way did not make it to Thailand. They were either killed or died in one way or another. People who escaped by boat, most from fishing villages. Fishermen were the only people who could use their boats to go to Malaysia, Singapore, Indonesia, the Philippines, Thailand, or Hong Kong.

Using fishing boats to escape was also extremely dangerous and difficult. The majority of those boats were no match for the high seas and huge waves. For that reason, a large percentage of the Vietnamese boat people became food for fish in the deep ocean. Aside from the difficult sea, many other factors that killed the boat people, and many of the escapees died before ever reaching free land. Arranging to escape by boat could be as simple as someone allowing you on a boat and leave the country or as complicated as making a connection with an organizer who planed the trip of escape. The organizer must have to decide the boat's capacity; how much each person must pay and the supplies of fuel, food, and water.

The organizer must also have to make a good team that must include experienced boat captain who could handle the boat on rough seas; boat pilot someone who knew about navigation; and more importantly, a good marine mechanic.

The price for each person was usually a few ounces of gold or tens of thousands of dollars. My mother began to explain how my brother escaped.

After the Fall of Saigon, my brother went to live with my sister in Vung Tau. Vung Tau was one of the popular locations from which people broke free from the Communist regime. Vung Tau is also one of the most beautiful places for vacationers. The coastal city is surrounds by peaks and valleys of hills and beaches, and the weather is pleasant year-round. Many fishing villages reside in this gorgeous city. When the wave of escapees began to flee the country, my brother also wanted to do just that. But he had no money or gold to pay to escape. He had to figure out the way. My sister referred him to a man she called the master of marine mechanics. My brother needed to become his student and follow the master and learn by on-hand training. After several months, he became a mechanic; then he got connected to one of the fishing boat owners. One day they escaped and made it to Thailand.

I was so happy for my brother. At the same time, I felt sad because I might never be able to see him again. But then I thought again. I had an idea. I might follow in his footsteps. But then I did not know if I could leave my parents behind. However, if I stayed and lived with the Communists, I would have no future, as the Vietcong kept pushing our family to the mud.

My oldest brother's successful escape from Vietnam opened a new road for me. The more I thought about my brother's newfound freedom, the more I wished I were with him. I wished I didn't have to live with the Vietcong. I had been suffering.

One time, I overheard a conversation between my parents. They were considering letting me go to the south and live with my sister. My sister might find the way for me. I was so excited when I heard that.

A few months later, my mother arranged the trip. She asked me to quit school now and go with her to Vung Tau. I had a few days to think. I had such mixed feelings. I loved my parents. I kept thinking that my parents one day would need me and I would not be here for them. My parents knew that I would feel bad about leaving them; they told me it wouldn't do them much good if I stayed here with them anyway. They really wanted me to go and have a future. I listened to them. I packed my bag and said good-bye to my parents, brother, and sisters. This was it. My very long journey to freedom began.

III

$\mathscr{I}$ arrived in Vung Tau. I was so happy to see my sister and her family; however, I had left behind a large part of my family. I had also left behind my school, my classmates, my poor home, and my beloved garden of potatoes and vegetables. After I had lived with my sister for a few days, she told me a lot of things that had been happening around her area. She especially told me that many of the Vietcong police patrolled all over this region. They knew this place was the prime target for people who wanted to flee the country. She told me I had to be careful and not to wander around or talk to any strangers. She also needed to go to the local police office to inform them that she had a brother visiting her family from Quang Ngai; otherwise, I would stay with her illegally and I could get arrested.

When things were settled down for my stay, my sister broke exiting news to me. She said she had arranged for her entire family and me to make our escape in the next few weeks. Because her husband was one of the private nurses for the village, my sister and her husband had a few connections. Her husband was also a former soldier of the Republic of South Vietnamese Army. He was a combat medic for years during the war and had helped save many of his fellow soldiers. To get out of the Communist regime was also his dream. He valued nothing more than he and his family—the couple had five children—living in freedom.

My brother-in-law, a South Vietnamese Army combat medic Soldier, at his bunker.

For me, I had just said good-bye to my family, and now I was about to say good-bye to my country. The emotions that swelled up in me were nearly too much for a young boy, who was just starting to grow into a man. I was a little depressed, but I knew that my priority was to get out of the Communist regime.

The time had arrived. We had to get ready for the trip of our lives. My sister's family of seven and I got into a small bus very early in the morning. It took us about forty-five minutes to get to a secret location. We walked into a house and to a large room. Here we were. My sister said we had to sit here in the room and wait until dark; then we might go to the beach and get on a boat. It was a long day for us. We were the first group to arrive. Then every few hours, there came another family.

The room was crowded by the end of the day. I realized that we didn't want to gather the crowd all at once. That way we wouldn't get much notice by the Vietcong forces or any people surroundings. We sat and waited and waited. The room had become small for that large number of people, including small children. We all grew very uneasy and anxious. Hopefully, all the patience would pay off and we would soon be ordered to go to the beach catching the escaping boat.

A man showed up around midnight and said we might go to the beach around two o'clock. The good news excited everyone. We thought this was the real deal, and we were informed the process was in progress. Those two hours of waiting were the longest and slowest two hours I had endured. We could not wait to get out of the room, go to the beach, and get on the boat. The anticipation was tremendous.

Soon, it was almost two o'clock in the morning. Everyone looked at the clock constantly. I kept staring at the door and wishing someone would open it and order us to go. Two a.m. passed, but no one opened the door. We remained patient and hoped for the best. Around two thirty, the man who'd appeared earlier showed up and told us the bad news. He said we couldn't go anywhere because the Vietcong marine police had had some suspicion and stopped the boat for questioning.

Disappointed flooded the room. I almost burst into tears; I thought this was my one opportunity of a lifetime to run away from the Communists. Now we had to go back home. We had to start leaving the room by dawn. We certainly didn't want the Vietcong to see that many of us gathered in a room like this. That would cause a lot of troubles. My sister's family and I returned back to her home that morning.

A few days later, my sister told me that we had been cheated. My sister had paid a small amount of money to make the deposit for our seats for the trip. Now she could not get the money back, and she knew the whole thing was just a setup. A lot of people tried to make money from other people this way at this time. The situation became very confused and complicated. I was very sad, but my sister talked to me and cheered me up somewhat. One thing that really made me happy was when she told me that, if she could not succeed in finding a way for everyone to escape, she would at least try her best to figure out a way for me to leave. I thanked her. I prayed for our escape to take place and I was willing to try and try again.

My strong will and determination led me to a series of problems and troubles. I was vulnerable, and a lot of predators lurked in waiting. Some deceived people in order to make money. Others were undercover Communists setting traps; they would take young people like me to the Vietcong's jail or make a lot of money from their captives' families.

My second opportunity soon arrived. My sister had just come back from the market, and she pulled me into a room. She told me she just met a good woman, whom she would trust, and the woman told my sister that a good group of people organized to leave the country tomorrow night. The woman told my sister that she would not ask for any money up front. She would tell the owner of the boat to let me on board and make the escape; then we would pay the boat owner when the boat making the escape successfully.

The situation sounded trustworthy, so my sister and I decided to take action. I had dinner with my sister's family, realizing this could be my last dinner with them. My brother-in-law wished me luck. Once again, I packed an extra set of clothes and mentally prepared myself. I had to leave my sister's house late in the morning and I took the ferryboat to the island where the escape would take place in the next early morning. I said good-bye to my sister and arrived at the island the afternoon. I met a few people, all of whom were very nice and friendly. They told me to chill out and wait after the sunset and then they would tell me what to do. I followed their instructions accordingly.

When the sky began getting dark, I followed a man to his canoe. He asked me to get on the canoe, and he took me to a shallow beach area that looked like a small jungle on water. He asked me to get off the canoe and told me to stand in the shallow water at this location and wait until a fishing boat passing by and picking me up. He said it might be just a few hours. Once again, I listened and followed instructions accordingly.

Here I was, alone in the middle of nowhere. It was pitch–black, and I could not see anything. Every now and then, I saw little lights from a distance on the water. Every time I spotted some lights, I would get extremely excited because I knew those lights belonged to fishing boats. I thought the boat would come to me and pick me up. Sadly, I was disappointed every single time. After standing there for an hour, nothing had happened and no boat came to me. As the night deepened, I grew more and more scared. I was here in the place that looked like a wild jungle of wilderness all by myself. Anything could happen here. Anybody could kill me, and no one would ever know. I became very cold from standing in the water for so long, and as the temperature dropped through the night, I started to think what was happening to me?

My sister had sent me here because she trusted her friend's connection and forgot about her own brother's safety. I could end up endangering myself in many different ways. As the high tide came, more of my body would be submerged, and I might become hypothermic. What about poisonous water snakes? They could kill too. So many frightening thoughts came to my mind all at once, I almost wanted to scream out loud, "Somebody, please help me!" But I didn't scream. I tried to hold my own. I closed my eyes, took deep breaths, and attempted to stabilize my thoughts. I needed to be smart and figure out the way to safety. A few hours had passed, but still no boat had arrived to pick me up.

It was almost midnight. I was freezing. I started moving my hands and rubbing my body to keep warm. Then my mind said that this was enough. I needed to get out of here before my body froze died in the water. I started to walk slowly to shallower water. I kept walking, even though I had no idea in what direction I should go. I got stuck in the mud and tripped a few times over the trees in the water.

Suddenly, I saw several lights from a far distance. I figured this was the light of the village on the island where I'd been before I was taken to this particular location. I was happy; now I knew what direction I should be heading. But from here to the village on the island could be very long because the lights looked so far away. I kept walking on the shallow water and mud toward the village but I had a hard time. It was so dark that I couldn't even see my steps.

Soon, I was exhausted, and I wished I had a place to sit and catch my breath. As I kept walking through mud and sea trees, the village got closer and closer. I eventually made it to dry land. I recognized the place where I'd come from. As I kept going, I remembered the house of the man with the canoe. Now it was about two o'clock in the morning. I knocked on the door and waited for a few minutes. The same man opened the door. He said he was surprised to see me back. He asked me what had happened. I simply told him that no boat had come to pick me up and I had figured out by myself how to get here. He let me in the house, and I washed up my muddy feet. He was also nice enough to let me sleep in his house for a few hours after having suffered the nightmare of standing in the water at the beach.

I caught the ferry and went back home to my sister's home that morning. My sister saw me with long face; she knew that something was seriously wrong. I sat in the room with her and told her I about my scary and horrible time. I was so happy that I was able go home and see my sister and her family. She felt very bad and sorry for me after listening to my account; at the same time, she was also very upset about that woman whom she'd trusted.

A few days later, my sister met the woman and had a lot questions for her. After a long meeting, my sister realized that she shouldn't trust that woman at all. With all the things considered, I put together the clues from my experience and my sister's conversation with that women, we determined the reason why the lady didn't ask for any money upfront because she was not honest enough but trying to be clever the way she would make money from the vulnerable escapees. She would try to help anyone to flee from the country when she might just happen to know by rumors that some group of people planned to escape in a particular location on the island. If anyone followed her instructions that happened to guide the person to the right place at the right time and, also, if the owner of the boat had the mercy to allow the person to get on the boat, then her plan would be a success. Otherwise, she was just nobody at all. This lady didn't belong to any organization; nor did she have any authority whatsoever. Her plans to help anybody escaped left the outcome up to chance or luck. That made my trip even more uncertain and dangerous. She played with people's lives.

She didn't want any money at the beginning because she was not sure about how things would turn out. If she got lucky that someone did really escape through her "plan," then she would go to the family and demand for a lot of money.

I poured so much of my energy and focus into getting away from the Communists. So far I hadn't succeeded, but I felt fortunate that I was safe and alive. But one day living with the regime was one day of sadness and hatred. I became very depressed. I didn't know what to do or what to think. My family was poor and could not afford to pay big money to any good organization for my escape. Even so, if we had the money, we still wouldn't know whom to trust and what kind of safety measures we would get involved. The situation was very complicated. I just had to close my eyes and pray to God. *"Please help me and lead me the way!"*

A few weeks after the last attempt of escape, something happened again. My sister and her husband had some other connection. Somehow this time, my sister really trusted these people. She even paid some money in advance and said she would pay the rest if my escape were a success. Seeing my sister's enthusiasm about this trip didn't necessarily lift my spirits, but it increased my faith. I had faith that, one day, God would help me run away from the one of the most brutal regimes on earth.

I listened to my sister and did whatever she asked me. I wholeheartedly thanked her for all she had done for me. I knew she wanted me to have a better future. She wanted me to have all the good things in life. She always trusted in me, especially since she knew that I was a good boy, who was smart and responsible and always wanted to go to school and learn to succeed, and help others.

Time had come for my third try. I got ready for the night, said good-bye to my sister and her family, and left the house. I took the bus to the address I'd been given. This time, the location was not too far away. It was only twenty minutes from my sister's home.

I arrived at the location, and a man let me in the house. He told me to just sit down and wait for the sunset. Then he would move me to a different location. The sun had set, and the lights of the street were turned on. The man told me to jump on his motorcycle. After a fifteen-minute ride, we arrived in a countryside village. He took me to a house. He said to just go into the room and stay there until somebody would take me to the beach where I'd meet my boat. I went in the room and saw sixteen people sitting down. I sat down with the group and started waiting.

I felt the atmosphere growing tensed and uneasy right away. People kept whispering to each other, anxious for the time when we'd get out of the room and go to the boat. I felt the same. I closed my eyes and started praying. I kept saying, *"Please, God, I have tried two times to escape, but both attempts have failed; please let me succeed this time."* I felt so much pain in my soul, and I noticed tears in my eyes.

After three hours of waiting, it was nearly midnight. Time passed so slowly, and it seemed like we could not wait anymore; however, we were whispering to each other to hold on and be patient. The tension was high in everyone's mind. Every minute that passed seemed a day of holding my breath. It was about one o'clock in the morning and the atmosphere became more intense. Something could happen anytime now.

Indeed, something happened. I heard some noise that sounded like somebody loading bullets into a gun chamber from the other side of the door. Then immediately the door busted open. Oh my God! A Vietcong policeman stood at the door holding an AK-47 in his arms.

"Run, run!" somebody shouted.

In a split second, I had stormed out of the room, reacting without thought. I ran out of the house. It was too dark. I couldn't see anything at all. It was just the darkness and I; but I had to run because I didn't want to get shot by that Vietcong. I ran and ran and ran, but I had no idea what direction I was running in. I ran for about ten minutes, and I tripped over a big piece of wood on the ground; then I realized I had run into a large pond full of water and long, wild grass. Out of breath, I panicked. I knew I was at the highest level of distress. In my mind, I immediately called up my parents to come and rescue me. I thought that I would die right here because I couldn't run anymore. I become so frightened that my mind went into an unconscious state. I saw the many Vietcong soldiers armed with AK-47s surrounding the pond and pointing their rifles at me. I immediately yelled out in my mind, *don't shoot!*

My eyes suddenly opened, and I realized I was still in the water.

I regained consciousness and tried to get out of the pond so I could run again. Once out, I continued running. I kept looking back, and I didn't see anybody following me. I calmed myself down and tried to gain control over the situation. Finally, I saw some lights moving from a distance. I figured that were some vehicles were on the road. I was so happy. I would reach the road and find my way home. I took deep breaths and tried to clean the mud from my feet so that I would look okay, just in case anyone stopped me. I reached the road and recognized my location. I walked slowly, finally arriving home around four o'clock in the morning. I stepped in my sister's house, woke her up, and then burst into tears. I held my sister and cried. I tried to let all the pain and terrifying thoughts out of my soul. I settled down and told my sister about the nightmare. She fixed me some soup, and I lay down to get some much-needed sleep.

I slept almost the entire day. I was still tired and exhausted. What else would happen to me? I was so depressed and discouraged. What should I do now? I kept asking myself that question, and I didn't know the answer. I just closed my eyes and continued to sleep.

Days came and went. I wanted to take it easy and forget about fleeing the country for now. I told my sister to let me stay home and clean the house for her. I got nervous every time I thought about what had happened to me; however, the reality of living with the Communists was very frustrating, and I had no future. I couldn't surrender my dream. I had to accept the fact that I might get killed, caught, or otherwise harmed when I took a chance and attempted to escape the Communists. In other words, I determined that I would rather die than stay with the Communists and face their reality.

As the going got tough; the tough got going. I thought of what I had been going through made me a tougher person. I had determined and made up my mind. I needed to follow my dream—my dream to be a free man no matter what was in front of me. I told my sister I would stand up and try again.

A few weeks later, my sister found another connection. She asked me to try, but I failed again. The difference this time was that the Vietcong didn't notice us. We were dismissed in an organized way before anything bad happened.

A month later, the head organizer of that attempt came to my sister house and let her know that they were going to try again in a few days. My sister asked me to join the group again. This attempt also failed. It was a good thing was that none of us were caught or harmed in any way. I considered myself very lucky.

I had tried five times to make my dream come true, but I hadn't gotten very far. For all of these times, I had never even seen the boat I might use to escape. I was really disappointed. I asked myself when I would be able to see the real deal. I wondered if this would ever happen for me.

IV

One day, my sister and I sat down and had a long talk. We wanted to explore some options. It was a good time for us to assess the probability and safety measures. At one point, our discussion turned to my brother's escape; his way had been the best method. He was a mechanic on the escaping boat, so he was a necessary part of the organization. This was a real deal, a real boat, and real people. The only downside to following in my brother's footsteps was that I would need to become a mechanic, and doing so would take a lot of time.

But I would take the time if it meant a better chance of successfully escaping the Communists. I didn't have to rush and fail. I wanted to make more careful plans—more sure ways. Most of all, I wanted to feel more safe and secure if the event was taking place. I thought this would be the best plan for me; one thing in my favor was that the master mechanic who had taught my brother was still around. Now our only worry was whether the master mechanic would accept me as his student.

Thank God, it happened. My sister asked the mechanic a few days after our discussion to allow me to be his student, and he said yes. I felt lucky and very happy.

A brand new chapter in my life began. I was excited to learn and meet people. I hoped and prayed that everything would turn out well. I started to play with tools and marine diesel engines. I knew that if I could learn to fix engines, I would become a mechanic and my new exciting adventures would begin.

The first few weeks were very tough for me. Every time I went on a boat and came into the engine room, I got extremely seasick. It took me a little while to adapt to the working conditions. Once I got over the tough working environment I really liked it. Fixing and seeing the broken engines run again were so much fun.

Things were going according to plan on my new course so far. However, I was now eighteen years of age, and I hadn't finished high school. I really missed the classroom atmosphere, friends, and my social life. One night at the family dinner table, my brother-in-law mentioned a program allowing his coworkers to continue their high school education at night. I asked him to help me so that I could join that program. I hoped I could get my high school diploma through night school and learn to be a mechanic during the days. My main focus still was getting trained as a good mechanic as soon as possible.

I made several friends. I was busy working and going to school every day, but I was happy. Day in and day out, I worked very hard. My master really liked me for my ability to learn. Sometimes he let me go and do a repair on my own. He started trusting in me and gave me responsibilities. I was very enthusiastic about taking any assignment from my master. I knew that I would soon become a good mechanic.

But one day, things didn't go right; I made a mistake that I gave him a wrong tool while he was doing the repair for one of the engines. I didn't do what my master wanted me to do. He got upset and threw a big tool that hit my head. The blow was very painful, but I still bounded down and respected him. I apologized to him.

My skills as a mechanic were really coming along. I got many compliments from many different fishing boat owners. Night school was also going well. I started have a social life. Some nights, my classmates and I would stay late on the beautiful Vung Tau beach and have a few cups of coffee.

One thing led to another, and before I knew it, I had developed feelings for one of the girls in my class. She really liked me too. We got along very well. Then the emotions kept building up. She said she was falling in love with me. I was very lonesome at the time. I lived with my sister, but I was miserable living without the rest of my family. Some days, when I would arrive home and my parents weren't there, sorrow would settle over me and nearly take my breath from me. My childhood had been broken so many times by the war, and now the Communist regime was doing the same thing to my life. Hearing this girl say she was falling in love with me warmed up my heart. She made me feel almost complete as a person—a man. We dated a few times a week, and grew ever fonder of each other. The love we had for each other developed every day.

Then one day, I realized that I needed to stop loving her and growing closer to her. Given my circumstances, one day I would be gone and would leave her behind. What would that be like for her? She would be miserable, and I didn't want to hurt her. Also being deeply in love with her might deter me from achieving my purpose of escaping the Communist regime, and I didn't want that to happen. I needed to stay focused on course to reach my dream. I had promised myself that nothing would change that. I had determined to seek freedom and liberty. I was humble to think that the love for liberation, for being a free man, was greater than the love I had for my first love. I still felt very sad because my feelings for her were very strong. I didn't want to reveal my whole truth to her about why I wanted to stop the relationship as soon as possible.

I didn't see her much anymore and we stopped dating. But she looked all over for me. She wrote me beautiful love letters. I felt sad and even loved her more when I read her letters. I just didn't know what to do. Besides, I had been hiding all of this from my sister. I didn't want her to know that I had fallen in love with a girl. I knew my sister would against it. She did not want me to get involved in any relationship because she was afraid it might affect my concentration—keep me from reaching my main goal. What she did not know was that I was very lonesome. I was very homesick for my parents and for the rest of the family.

After reading those letters from my girlfriend, I had to see her to see if she was doing okay. When we met, we talked and laughed together again. We both tried to stabilize our souls. We promised each other not to talk about sad things anymore, at least for now. We dated again, and one night she said she'd had a new idea. She told me she wanted to escape with me. She also wanted to be free. She said it would be her dream to seek freedom with me. Her father had also served as a South Vietnamese soldier, and her family was also suffering as a result of the new government.

It would be so awesome if we could escape together. But that was easier said than done. I had been struggling so much just to try and find a way on my own. In our situation of no money, having two persons escaping would be extremely difficult. But we could dream; hopefully, both of us could figure out the way.

Together, we climbed a hillside to a temple. We prayed for our dream to come true.

I continued my normal days. I had been developing my skills as a mechanic for several months already, and I felt I was coming along really well. I believed I should have the confidence to be on my own as a diesel engine mechanic. Most of all, I thought I was ready to take the responsibility to work with any people who wanted to organize a team to escape the country. One day, I asked my master if he thought I was ready to depart from him and be on my own. He said yes and he was very proud of me. I had become a good mechanic in such a short period of time. I appreciated my master so much. I would always remember him.

I was on course to make my dream come true. The business of boat engine repairs was getting busier every day. At the same time, a lot of people noticed me as a good mechanic. One day, a man came to my master and asked for help to find a good mechanic. My master immediately asked me if I wanted to work with the man. I was so happy to say yes to my master because I knew this was the real deal. I closed my eyes and said thanks to God; finally, things were going my way.

My dream was still alive. My real opportunity had arrived. I needed to get ready mentally and physically to flee from the Vietcong again. I called this "My Journey to Freedom Act II." I was so excited. I could not wait to see my own actions taking place. This time would be totally different from those previous times. I had become an important part of the real team. I would put on a huge responsibility by taking charge of the engine. I made sure I did my job and did it right, allowing for absolutely no margin of error.

If I made any mistake, the fates of a hundred of people would turn upside down; if, along our escape route, the engine stopped running, the consequences would be more terrible than anyone could imagine.

I had heard countless stories about the fates of boat people whose engines were malfunctioned and broken. Those boats became floating crafts on the high seas that got robbed, raped, and killed the people on the boat by the Thai pirates. Other boats got capsized as a result of engine not working, succumbing to the giant waves of the deep ocean, and the people drowned in the unforgiving high seas. One time, one boy somehow hung on to a wooden board and stayed afloat in the water for days. He finally drifted back to the coast of Vietnam and was still alive. Other stories told that the boat became a trap for the people. The Vietcong caught and arrested everyone on board because the boats whose engines had stopped running and it didn't go very far. These stories frightened me. But I could do this; I knew that I could take the responsibility and get the job done. I determined that if I installed, repaired, or took care of any engine, I promised myself that my engine would perform and run smoothly throughout the course.

I met the head organizer and went with him to the location where the boat was. He showed me the brand new wooden boat and then took me to the engine room. I saw no engine standing at this time but the engine parts were scattered all over the engine room. He asked me to do whatever it took to put the engine together and make it run. He gave me some money for whatever parts and supplies I would need to buy. He asked me to get it done in two weeks so he could put the entire plan together. I got a little dizzy when I saw the engine in such way. The pieces of metal strewn about the engine room made me nervous. I calmed myself down and told the man I would get into the business, and start working on the engine the next day. He looked at me in the eyes and encouraged me that he knew I could do it. He said he could rely on me. I felt much better when I heard those words. He had increased my confidence that I had the ability to get this most important task done. I knew that I faced the ultimate challenge.

Tomorrow had come. I gathered all my tools and supplies and went to work. Indeed, it didn't take long for me to figure everything out. I worked on the engine for less than a week, and every part of the engine was in its place. I took my time and installed one piece at a time carefully. In fact, I enjoyed the process of building up the engine. I called this an art—an art of making something out of nothing, of transforming pieces of metal into a powerful engine. I was very happy, and now I had to do the final check and make sure every piece was properly installed before I would be ready to start the engine for the very first time. Nervously, I turned to my helper, who had assisted me throughout the process. He was a good friend, and he'd kept me going. I just asked him if he thought I was ready to start the engine. He looked at me with an encouraging smile and said that he had no doubt the engine would run like a bird would sing. I thanked him and asked him to get out of the engine room and join me for a good break before we started the engine.

We both were ready for the moment of truth. I became so nervous; this was the first time I had installed an entire engine by myself without the supervision of my master. I closed my eyes, and I prayed to God, *"Please let the engine run."*

My assistant and I returned to the engine room. I made sure for the last time that the fuel and oil were in place. Then I cranked the engine for the first time. Out of the empty space, I heard the first loud noise of the engine. Then the noise calmed down to a good sound—the sound I was waiting to hear.

"It runs! It runs," my friend shouted.

We both left the room jumping up and down and celebrating the success. That was one of the happiest moments of my life; what a wonderful feeling it was. I stepped back into the engine room to double-check everything while the engine was running. Everything looked good except for a minor problem at the exhaust fitting; a small amount of smoke leaked from the pipe in the engine room, but that was an easy fix.

It was time to celebrate. My helper and I went out that night to a very small, local restaurant. We ate, we laughed, we drank, and we got drunk. I told my friend that I could not wait to tell the head organizer that my job was done, and I was ready for him to make the big plan. Furthermore, I couldn't wait to tell my master, as he would be so proud of me. I wanted to thank him a thousand times from the bottom of my heart. Lastly, I also wanted to tell my girlfriend about my recent success.

My opportunity to escape was getting closer and I knew that my girlfriend wanted to escape with me. I hadn't told her anything in my mind because I was afraid that the organizer wouldn't let my girlfriend to join me. I wanted to wait for the right time so that I could ask the organizer to allow me to take my girlfriend. The right time hadn't arrived yet, so all I wanted to tell my girlfriend was that I had successfully installed an engine on my own for the first time so that she would be proud of me.

Days went by, and I finally got the news from the organizer that we would have to be ready to launch the escape in a week. He came and talked with me and inspected the engine. I started the engine and ran the boat briefly for him to see. He was very pleased and happy with the performance of the engine. He asked me to stock all the necessary supplies for maintaining the engine and checked everything for final preparations.

I took this opportunity to talk with him about my girlfriend. It was a very hard subject for me to broach. Even though I was a mechanic now, I still felt I needed the organization more than it needed me. Besides, I was just a young man, and I didn't know the man well enough. I found it very difficult for me to find the words. However, the power of love gave me the bravery to speak to the man. I told him that I was involved in a relationship and I loved my girlfriend. I asked him if he would be kind enough to allow my girlfriend to escape with me.

He thought for a few minutes and then he apologized, saying that he had no more seats available and he could not allow an extra person on board. But he said he would give me some money to leave behind for the job well done. I respected his decision, and I told him it was okay. I closed my eyes, and I felt pain in my heart, even though I had mentally prepared for the negative answer. I was sad, but I had to move forward with the plan without telling my girlfriend.

My girlfriend and I, when we just started dating.

Soon, the escape was just a few days away. I told the organizer that I needed to go home to see my family for the last time. I went home and saw my sister and her family. I told my sister that this was it—that I was going to make the most important trip of my life and that I might not come back. I also told her that I was going to make the escape on a boat whose engine had been built by her own brother's hands. She was very impressed and happy for me.

I went and saw my girl friend that night. My heart was sadden, as I knew this might be the last time I saw her, though she didn't know it. We met each other at the Vung Tau beach, our usual and familiar place. It was a beautiful night with the bright stars and moon in the clear sky. We sat down on a big rock near the water. She was in my arms, and we listened to the waves cracking against the sand and the rock. After listening to the sounds for a little while, they became so familiar that they turned into the regular rhythm of music, blending with the beating of our hearts while we both remained silence. I wanted to say the words from my soul: *My sweetheart, I love you, but I have to leave you.* The achy feeling was spreading from my heart to my soul.

Although I didn't say those words, she still noticed the sadness in my eyes. She asked me to tell her what was wrong, and I just shook my head and told her that I had missed her so much. We were in each other's arms for a few final hours but we didn't say anything much. I didn't want the night to end, but it was too late already. I gave her a big, long kiss and told her we had to go home. She listened and grasped her bike, and I grasped mine.

We rode our bikes in the same direction until the direction was splitting. I asked her to stop the bike for a second. I went to her and gave her another kiss and said good-bye. She continued riding her bike alone while I stood watching her disappear into the night. I felt so much pain in my heart and soul. I noticed some drops of tears in my eyes.

V

After saying good-bye to my sister and her family, I took the bus and arrived at my boat the next morning. So much was going through my mind. I was very confident that we were going to successfully escape this time. Because I was the mechanic of the boat, I had the real sense that this actually going to happen. I could only remain in my country for one more day. Tomorrow night, we would take the boat out and make the escape. I counted down the time, hour by hour. I felt depressed knowing that I left so much behind.

The time had come. We took the boat out via a small canal. It was about nine o'clock in the evening. The boat reached a bigger body of water and then the ocean. We pretended to fish while we waited for the right time and signals. By midnight, we took the boat back to the canal. Here the boat went slowly; we were searching for connecting signals from smaller boats. Three people and I were the only people on the boat at this time. The captain was the only one steering the boat. The other two were working on the signals, and I paid attention to the running engine. As far as I understood, we were supposed to load the fuel, water, and food supplies by twelve thirty and load people on board by one o'clock.

As the boat moved slowly along, everyone's heartbeats raced anxiously, waiting for something to happen. By twelve thirty, we still had no signal. We went back and forth in that appointed canal several times, waiting for any signal. Soon it was close to one o'clock, and we still saw nothing.

Suddenly, a small light flashed in the distance. That was it. We were all excited and scared at the same time. We reached the small boat and saw only two people on it. They broke the bad news. The Vietcong had noticed the area where we were hiding the passengers. As a result, the organizer had had to dismiss the group before the Vietcong police caught them. The two people on the small boat asked us to move our boat to the big water and continue pretending to fish.

Oh my God! I was so disappointed. I wanted to scream from the top of my lungs. The captain immediately followed the order before it got too late. He turned the boat around and went to the ocean. We waited for the sunrise so he could turn the boat back home.

The sun was up, and we headed back home. When we arrived home, a few people (other organizers) came to the boat and talked to us. They told us to just make believe nothing had happened and try to get some rest and wait for the new order from the organization. It had been a long night, and I was exhausted. I ate some soup, obtained a small blanket, and lay down in the cabin of the boat. I got some sleep.

I woke up in the afternoon. Everything seemed very quiet and normal. I saw the captain and asked him what we were going to do. He said that tomorrow night we would have to go pretend fishing again and wait for the new set of orders.

We took the boat out and went fishing the next night. Along the way, we tried to learn more about these small canals and we explored the beach area further. We wanted to be more prepared and ready when the time would come.

Then there came a new order from the organization. We needed to get ready again in the next four days. I asked permission to go back to my sister's home for a day. I wanted to let her know what was going on so she wouldn't worry. When I arrived home, she was very surprised. I told her what had happened and I let her know that we would try again in three days.

I also wanted to visit my girlfriend. I rode my bike to her workplace. I asked her if we could see each other on the beach that night. We met at the same place and shared the evening that I thought it would never happen again. I was so happy to meet her. I tried not to be sad like the last time we met. Once again, my girl was back in my arms. I tried to forget everything else and just enjoy the quality time with the one I loved. We drank coffee, we talked, and we laughed for the whole night. As the night was getting late, we said good-bye, and I told her I would see her in a few days, although I didn't know what would be going to happen on the next several days.

The next morning, I said good-bye to my sister and took the bus to my boat. Here we were again, trying to prepare mentally and physically for the trip. We took the boat out and pretended to fish that night. We trapped a lot of shrimp. My dinner was fresh grilled shrimp with lemon and salt. The practice night went very well. We only had one more night, and then, hopefully, the action of our lives would take place.

The night arrived. We needed to get ready to take the boat out. Before I cranked the engine, I touched the head of the engine and prayed, *"Please… help me make this escape."*

I mustered up all my confidence. I started the engine and signaled the captain to start moving the boat out. It was ten o'clock in the evening. The boat started moving slowly, and we all started getting the anxiety. The plan of attack was almost the same as it had been the last time. We would pick up the fuel, food, and water around midnight and the people at about one o'clock. Then we would head out to open sea. We were out to the big body of water around eleven o'clock. We pretended to fish until midnight. Then we moved into the designated canal. We started looking for signals.

Before long, we received signals from the small boats. Everything was looking good according to the plan thus far, and we met with three small boats with supplies. We took the fuel, food, and water on board. One of the men on the small boat told us to just hang tight for half an hour; they would deliver passengers to us.

The three small boats disappeared, and we circled the same area, waiting for the people to come on board. We waited and we waited. Thirty and then forty minutes passed. We still didn't see anything. Now we were getting worried. The captain told us to remain calm and patient.

Now an hour of waiting passed and we still didn't have any people on board. In my mind, something was seriously wrong. This long period of waiting couldn't be right when they had told us only thirty minutes.

Suddenly, we saw one signal from one small boat. We immediately came close and asked what had happened. One man told us that we were in deep trouble. The Vietcong police had arrested a number of passengers. The man told us that we needed to get the boat out of the area and we needed to leave the boat as soon as possible after we took the boat home because the Vietcong would eventually look for the boat.

I almost had a heart attack. I couldn't believe this was happening to me once again. Now I had no time to think about anything else but my safety. I certainly didn't want to get caught by the Communists. We had the obvious evidence of the fuel, food, and water on the boat, and if the Vietcong inspected the boat, there was no way they would let us go. The captain said that we would head back to the boat dock and then we all had to abandon the boat right away.

We all agreed. We were so anxious and worried that the Vietcong police might be waiting to arrest us at the boat dock. At just past two o'clock in the morning now, we approached the boat dock. We constantly looked around, trying to see or hear anything through the darkness of the night.

I looked up toward the dark sky and prayed to God, "*Please don't let the Vietcong catch me.*"

The boat arrived at the dock, and everything seemed quiet.

"*Let's leave the boat right now,*" the captain said.

"*Please wait for me, just one minute,*" I replied.

I came in the engine room; I touched the engine, saying good-bye. I spoke with the engine, "*I took care of you so well, but now I have to leave you.*" Then I quickly grabbed my tool bag and left.

Then all four of us jumped off the boat. We walked away quickly, planning to go to the home of one of the three men. It was about a twenty-minute walk, but we all still worried that we might see any Vietcong along the way. We had no choice but to keep walking and hope for the best.

We arrived at the man's house at about three o'clock. We saw his family, and we wanted to stay there and rest for a few hours after a long night. We sat down and talked for several minutes, and some concerns came up. The family of the man said it wouldn't be a good idea for us to stay in the house because the local Vietcong might come here. The family suggested that we should keep walking to the bus station, and if anybody asked, we should say we wanted to catch the first early bus to another city.

The three of us said good-bye to the man and his family, and we walked for about forty minutes to the bus station. Fortunately, no one stopped us for anything. At this time, it was still very early, and the station was very empty and quiet, but we thought we were very much safe. I was extremely tired because I had carried my tool bag. I just lay on the floor in a corner and passed out.

Suddenly, I heard some noise. My eye slowly opened and saw people around me. I was panicked and scared for a second, thinking that the Vietcong had caught me. I closed my eyes for a few seconds and opened them again. I realized that I was being paranoid by the thinking of Vietcong were looking for me. It was dawn now and people were there to wait for their buses.

I finally took the bus home to my sister's very early in the morning. Now I thought I would be out of the woods—the Vietcong wouldn't catch me. I stepped in the house after my sister opened the door. She couldn't believe it when I told her what had happened. She gave me a big hug and thanked God that I had successfully ran from the Vietcong. She was happy that I was safe, and she said she was going to prepare a good dinner to cheer me up.

Depression descended on me because I kept losing the hope. I had so much confidence that I would be able to make the escape this time. How many more times should I continue trying to get away from the Communists before I could actually make it? I just couldn't understand what was going on with my life. I had prayed so much, and I still I couldn't succeed. I thought I had no doubt that I should be able to find the real deal and escape once I became a mechanic. Everything I'd believed had proved to be untrue, and I just didn't know what to believe. I was desperate, and I had no idea what I should do.

Over the next few days, I learned that the Vietcong had towed my boat away. We had lost everything. We had invested so much time and money into the boat, and now it was in the Communist's possession. I got sick in my stomach to think that my engine, which I had cared for so much, was gone. I also learned the owner of the boat and a few other members in the organization were arrested. I was so lucky to have gotten away, but I still worried that the Vietcong would be looking for me.

I made myself scarce for the next several days. I was afraid that the Vietcong might go to my sister's home and look for me. Some days, I wandered on the Vung Tau beach and spent time with my girlfriend. On other days, I was in different locations.

When all remained quite, I believed I had escaped the incident unharmed. I went back to my sister's house and started working with my master again.

Several weeks passed. I was glad to be working with my master once again. I always tried to improve my mechanic skill. I was exposed to different kinds of diesel engines. I felt more comfortable with what I did. My goal was to become one of the best mechanics in this fishing village. I knew that, in order for me to become popular and a great mechanic, I had to be really reliable, dependable, knowledgeable, and responsible. I thought I had no problem doing that. I worked very hard. I built my work ethic on good morality. I treated people with respect and dignity. One day, I hoped, good things would happen to me.

VI

Indeed, one day I met a man. He came to my master and asked if my master could find him the best mechanic. I was there at the time they met; and my master introduced me to him and said, *"Here is your best mechanic."*

I shook the man's hand and told him my name. He invited me to a restaurant for lunch so we could get to know each other. It turned out that he was one of the former high-ranking police officers of the former South Vietnamese government. He had suffered a great deal in the Communist camps and had done hard labor in the Communist prison after the Fall of Saigon. His determination to escape the grips of the regime was clear. He had a large family, and he wanted his whole family to escape.

The man started telling some progress of his plan. He said that the wooden boat being built at this time. Now, He wanted to shop for an engine for the boat. We had a long conversation and I highly respected him for what he had suffered and gone through. We seemed we were very happy with each other. He accepted me to come on board with his plan. He asked me that I should join him to shop for a good engine in Saigon city in a few days. He also told me that he had a son about my age. He would tell his son to help me when I started installing the engine. I broke a friendly smile with him and told him that it would be an honor for me to join his team.

I met the man two days later, and we went to Saigon to look for the engine. He told me he had some connections for finding a good diesel engine on the black market. I just followed him, and we finally found a big engine that he really liked. He told me this engine would match with the boat. He finalized the deal and scheduled to have the engine delivered in a few days to the boat's location.

A few days later, I started the engine installation process. Here I was to start the process all over again. I was feeling good and I was excited to see the brand new boat with a brand new engine. The boat was much larger than the previous one; the same was true for the engine. This would be my first time installing the engine of this kind. I also had a good helper, the owner's son. He seemed nice, and we got along very well. I unpacked my toolbox and set out to organize an array of nuts and bolts and engine parts.

Good thing the engine room was very large; that made my work much easier. However, I was panicking just by looking at hundreds of engine parts that had to be put together; I tried to stay calm because I knew I could do this. I wanted to strengthen my confidence to overcome any obstacle of the installation process. Even though, this engine was much larger of different kind, the basic principle was the same. I had done this before, and I could do it again, even better.

Indeed, with the hard work and the greatest effort, in a week, the engine was nicely installed, and we were ready for the very first crank. The first spark of a newly installed engine was always a special moment for me. I was very anxious, under a lot of stress and pressure to see if the engine could run after I thought I was done with the installation. I asked my friend if he thought we were ready to start the engine. He looked at me with a smile and said that he had no doubt. I told him to get out of the engine room and take a break. He invited me to smoke a cigarette so I could relax and ease my mind a little bit.

We went back down to the engine, and I did the final check before starting the engine. I had my friend make the crank while I was checking and inspecting the engine. Suddenly, the engine's first big noise occupied the empty space, like the first cry of a newborn baby. I was so excited; I shouted to my friend, *"It runs. It runs!"*

Wow! I could not describe the great feeling. I did the final tune-up, and the engine ran even smoother. I told myself I did it again.

Things were very much in place. The owner was very pleased with the engine, and he shared with me that the action was to take place in just a few weeks. His son helped me to make all the preparations for the trip. Once again, we would pretend to go fishing for a short while before we would make the escape. I felt better this time than I had the last time. My experience had built up my confidence. Besides, I had better times and enjoyed the atmosphere much more than before. After a hard day of work, the boat owner's son and I went out to nightclubs. We seemed to understand each other very well. One time, he got his girlfriend, and I got mine, and the four of us went out together. We were delightful of each other's company. The climate of friendship turned out to be much better than I expected.

The day of the plan was getting closer. My mind was on my girlfriend all the time. I thought this would be a better opportunity for me to demand a seat for my girlfriend. However, I didn't want to be too strong in my demand with the owner. I approached my friend and asked him to ask his father and I hoped the owner would allow my girlfriend to come on board with me.

A day later, the son told me that his father had agreed—my girlfriend could come with me. I was so happy. Our dream of escaping together might come true. I couldn't wait to tell her.

I had to go home right away. First, I needed to say good-bye to my sister and her family, and then I needed to tell my girlfriend the great news. She would need to prepare for the escape because it was only several days away.

I met her and shared the good news. She was ecstatic. She gave me a big hug, and I noticed tears in her eyes. I asked her to come to the location in two days prior the day of escape. Then I would contact her to tell her what to do next. She listened, and I went back to my sister's home for the last supper with her family, I hoped.

I felt bad about not telling my sister that my girlfriend may accompany me on the escape. I wasn't sure why, but I got the feeling that she didn't want me to get involved in a relationship with anyone. Perhaps she was afraid that I would get into more trouble and or lose my focus.

I said good-bye to my sister and went back to my boat the next morning. My friend and I tried to make the final preparations. We had made a few pretend fishing trips and had become familiar with the routes. I had bought some more necessary spare engine parts, along with a few additional water pumps. I felt very good about our preparations and we thought we were all ready for the escape of our lives.

It was a beautiful afternoon, and I stood on the top front of my beautiful boat, still not quite believing where I was—atop a magnificent fishing boat with a powerful engine that I had built with my own hands. This boat with this engine would carry more than a hundred escapees to the high sea in searching for a new land of freedom. This time, included among the escapees would be my girlfriend and I. More than ever, I prayed for the escape to be successful. The future held so much in my dreams.

My friend interrupted my thoughts. "*Hey, mechanic!*" he called. "*Let's get ready to go fishing.*"

I turned my attention to my friend, the boat captain, and two others jump onto the boat. We pretended to go fishing again tonight for the last time.

We took the boat out while some daylight remained. I looked far on the horizon and saw the sun was just about to set. The beautiful, clear sky blended with the last weak sunlight of the day that shone on the reflected image of the pink clouds in the crystal clear, calm water made the evening so magical. My country was so beautiful. Wishing I could physically hug my country in my small arms, I whispered, "*I love you so much.*" If the Communist regime hadn't conquered my country, I wouldn't leave her for anything. A few sad moments came up in my soul.

We caught a lot of shrimp that night and my favorite—grilled shrimp dipped in salt and lemon juice. We enjoyed the night out very much. The captain then turned the boat home. We didn't want to spend too much energy that night. If things went according to plan, tomorrow night would be the night of action.

We got the boat back to the dock very early in the morning. I tried to get some sleep. I wanted to be well rested and preserve energy for the next few days. I slept like a baby for a few hours, until something disturbed my slumber. "*Mechanic, wake up.*" It was my friend, waking me so we could get ready for tonight.

He told me to get my girlfriend and take her to a specific location where the boat would pick her up. I immediately went to see my girlfriend. She was staying in her cousin's house, which was nearby. It only took me fifteen minutes to ride to her place. I met her, and she said she had been waiting for me for so long. She was very anxious and worried for me. I told her that I had been waiting for the owner's order and I also explained to her about the pick-up location. She climbed on the back of my bike. When we arrived at the location, I told the person in charge the secret code so he would let my girlfriend in. I said good-bye to her, wished her luck, and asked her to pray hard for everything to go smoothly. I had to get back to the boat, get ready before sunset.

Back at the boat, the crew was all there. The captain, my friend, and the other two fishermen gave firm handshakes. We wished good luck to each other in our voice.

The sun had almost set, and it was time to set the plan into action.

"Let's start the engine and go fishing," the captain said.

I followed the order and stepped down to the engine room. I looked at my engine and whispered, *"You are a magnificent engine; please help me get through my mission."* I cranked the engine, and a joyful noise filled my ears. The captain happily took the boat out.

The plan tonight was very similar to that of my previous trips. The primary difference was that this boat was much larger and we had to be extra careful when running through small canals. We certainly didn't want to get stuck in the shallow water, especially not tonight. We would load the fuel, food, and supplies around midnight and then load the people shortly thereafter. Time seemed to pass very slowly. We all were very anxious for tonight. For me, knowing that my girlfriend would be with me on the trip heightened both my anxiety and my excitement. I hoped and prayed that all would go smoothly.

At nearly midnight, we moved in to the smaller canal, looking for contact signals. We looked and looked but saw nothing. Thirty minutes passed and then an hour. The silence filled the air with all the anxiety and worries. We wondered if there was anything wrong with the process.

After two hours had passed and we still had no contact, the captain mentioned that we had to get out of the canal. We had been circling in this area for too long. We didn't want to get suspicious if any Vietcong boat saw us. Knowing that something had definitely gone wrong, we had no choice but to move the boat into open water and pretend to fish for the rest of the night.

We turned the boat back home very early in the morning. I couldn't wait to find out what had happened. It turned out that the boat owner's nerves had nearly given him a heart attack. Lacking the bravery required to take the chance, he'd called off the action.

I got off the boat as soon as we'd docked and went looking for my girlfriend. I found her at her cousin's home, and she was okay. She told me that the people in charge at the secrete location had simply dismissed everyone, telling them to return home. I saw some sadness in her eyes. I told her not to worry and to go back home to Vung Tau; we would do this again when the right time come. She understood; I gave her a big hug, and we said good-bye.

Exhausted, I returned to the boat. I needed to rest. I also wondered what would happen next. That evening, I received a very bad news. The local Vietcong had come to the owner's house and taken him to their office for questioning. The Communists had, somehow, learned something of last night's escape attempt. They had some evidence to accuse the owner's movements against the Communist regime, and they arrested him. As soon as I heard the bad news, I packed up my tools and went back home to my sister's. I knew that the Vietcong might come to the boat and look for me.

When my sister saw me arriving home at nighttime, her eyes opened wide in shock and she asked me what on earth had happened. I shook my head and told her that nothing was good. I had failed to make the escape once again. She understood my frustration. She tried to comfort me and said that it could have been worse. She was thankful to see me home safely. I guessed she was right. I needed to see the glass half full, but not half empty. The road I passed through had been so bumpy, but I had to stand up and try and try until I succeeded. I wanted to make my mind clear. I would never stop trying to escape the Communists until I died, and I would rather die than to live with the Communist regime.

I took a few days to relax. I soon learned that the Vietcong had towed my boat away after arresting the owner. My magnificent engine was now gone. The loss was so devastating I couldn't stop thinking about it. My hopes were so high, my dreams were so big, and in a flash, both hopes and dreams had disappeared. Who knew what my future would hold?

I went to see my girlfriend and spend some time with her. We tried to find comfort in each other's company and forget about reality. Once again, we enjoyed the ocean's song, the bitterness in the cup of coffee, and the laughter when we made fun of each other.

VII

$\mathcal{I}$got back to my normal routine after the big disappointment. My master loved to see me back and working with him, even though he always wished me the best of everything. I always respected him, like my own father. I appreciated more than I could tell him what the best teacher he was.

The normal days came and went. About two months after I'd returned, I got another connection. This time two men came looking for a mechanic. In fact, these two men knew about me. They came from the same area where I had worked on the last boat, and they knew the previous owner. They had come to look for my master because they didn't know where I lived. We made the connection easily when they saw me with my master. We then got to know each other very quickly.

Interestingly, it was time for me to do what I did again in the same area but different owner. I had spent quite some time in the region and had gotten to know a number of people. My friends and the boat's owner even gave me a nickname—the Mechanic. Now I would be dealing with a similar process but different people. As I understood, the two owned the boat jointly. They both were former South Vietnamese officers and they seemed more aggressive and bravery than the previous owner. They both also had beautiful, large families. They revealed to me that these two men had more determination and better organization. Somehow, I had more confidence in this escape than ever before. The boat and the engine were a bit smaller but it was still a good size.

Now this would be the third time I had built and installed an engine on my own. I thought I had become a very decent mechanic by now. I knew everything about the engine from inside out. I noticed that people paid me better respect. I couldn't be more proud of myself. I thought that, this time, I shouldn't have a problem asking the owners straight out about a seat for my girlfriend when the time came. I also hoped this would be the last time I tried to escape; but I also didn't want to make my hopes too high because I might then be so disappointed if I didn't make the escape like many times before. I reminded myself to put everything in perspective.

I became more popular and I had more friends than ever before. I enjoyed the hospitality and support of many people in the village. They made me feel like I was a part of their real families. I appreciated the way they treated me. They liked me because of my honesty and I always gave my work 100 percent effort of my work contribution.

It was time for me to ask the owners' permission to take a few days off so I could go home and visit my sister's family. They gave me the okay, mentioning also that the day of action was close—only about two weeks. They asked me to prepare and check on everything when I get back. I wanted to tell them about my girlfriend, but somehow I couldn't say anything yet. I took off for Vung Tau.

I arrived at my sister's home very late in the afternoon. I had been gone for about three weeks, so I really missed my sister's family. I suggested that we needed to take te whole family out for dinner. My sister agreed, and we had a great evening. During the dinner, I sat next to my sister and reported to her all the progress we were making and the plan of attack in the days to come. I told her I might be trying to escape again in two weeks. I also told her that I somehow sensed that, this time, the escape should be successful. She was very happy and proud of the work I had done. But as we talked, I noticed concern in the corners of her eyes. When I asked her if anything was the matter, she said she wanted to talk to me when we got home—that she'd have more to say to me then.

We got home, and my sister pulled me into a room. She asked me to sit so she could express all her concerns. She said it had been very rough for her and her husband to take care of their own family. Since the Communists had taken over, the economy worsened, corruption flourished and the revolution of escape from South Vietnam was growing larger and larger everyday. She knew of so many tragedies for the boat people because of bad organizations. She also knew that many people drowned in watercrafts that were no match with the sea. She named many other problems. For that reason, she said I had the best chance of success when I was the mechanic of the boat and I had become a part of the best organization. She said the opportunity that I had was rare.

She then came to the final point—she asked me to help her. She wanted her husband and oldest son, who was about six years old, to escape with me. She knew that I was a good mechanic now and I would be an important part of the team. She asked me to talk with the owners and ask them to allow me to have my brother-in-law and my nephew as the whole package.

Wow! I couldn't believe what I was hearing. My sister was willing to break her own family so that her husband could flee the Communist country. She obviously didn't have the money to buy the seats for her family to escape. I was saddened to see what people could to do in times of desperation. This was what the Vietcong did. Besides killing and brutalizing the South Vietnamese people, the regime was also the cause of many broken families in many different ways. How would her young children live without a father? She still had four children with her and how would she survive?

She remarked that her husband belonged to the former South Vietnamese Army and her dream was to have her husband go to America after escaping. He would find a job, work hard, and send her money home to support their family. She spoke to me in a sad tone indicating that she was desperate and couldn't tolerate the hard life with the Communist regime anymore. I still thought that when the man of the house left the family, I really worried that how she would be able bear her responsibility at home.

At the same time, I also thought of my girlfriend. This tore my heart out. I knew I couldn't have it both ways. I loved my girlfriend and we might plan a future together, but my sister's family was also very important to me. Furthermore, I had gotten where I was today because of the help of my sister. Without my sister, I wouldn't be here in Vung Tau. Without my sister, I wouldn't have had the opportunity to become a boat mechanic. Without my sister, I wouldn't have had a single chance to escape the Communist regime. So, I was thankful to her for many things.

Now she asked for my help; I knew that I had to do all I could to repay her. It was the sole opportunity for my redemption. After listening to my sister, I wanted to be sure that she had made her decision. She looked at me and said yes without hesitation. I told her that I would try my very best to make her wish come true. It had become very late at night. I needed some rest, and I told my sister not to worry.

I couldn't sleep much that night. So many thinking kept circling in my mind. I really needed to straighten out my thoughts, but I was still brokenhearted to take my girlfriend out of the picture. I didn't want my sister to know that. I didn't want things to get more complicated than they already were. On the other hand, I really wanted my girlfriend to know that I had a greater responsibility for my sister, now more than ever. She was a strong woman who made a lot of crucial decisions. She was the backbone of our large family.

I went to see my girlfriend the next night. I tried to keep everything normal, as if it were just another day. I had to keep the truth to myself. I truly believed that, if I were to tell her my decision, she might be very sad but she would understand and agree with me. I knew that my girlfriend was a smart girl who had a lot of good qualities and an open mind. I just didn't want to face reality. At the same time, I needed to be focused mentally and physically for the escape. I met her at the beach, and we made normal conversation. She noticed that something bothered me and asked me if I wanted to tell her. I told her that I was just tired from work.

I went back to the boat the next day. I worked on getting the boat ready so we could go fishing in the next few days. At the same time, I waited for the opportunity to talk to the owners about my brother-in-law and my nephew. I hoped they would agree with my proposal. I would mention that my brother-in-law was a South Vietnamese medic soldier. He might help sick people on the boat during the escape. I prayed good things would happen for my sister's family.

The boat was ready, and the engine was running smoothly. We pretended go fishing once again. Now I knew that I had to start the whole procedure of pretending all over again.

The night went fairly well. We returned to the village port early in the morning. I reported to the captain that the engine ran flawlessly. We continued to go fishing the next several nights. I thought we were very much ready for the action.

We took a night off. The owners came to the boat and asked us to go to one of their houses and have dinner with them. I might take this opportunity to speak with the owners about my sister's plan. I really had to prepare to talk with them. What I needed to tell them was that, if they needed me, I would ask them to open their hearts to allow my brother-in-law and my nephew to join me for the escape. I knew that we only had about another week on the plan, so I had to convey the message tonight.

Indeed, when the dinner was over, I waited for the last person to leave. I asked the owners to keep sitting so I could have a little talk with them, and then I just told them what I planned to say. They both seemed very considerate and understanding, and they said yes to my proposal. I was so happy, and I couldn't wait to tell my sister. I thought God had answered her prayer.

I went back to Vung Tau the next morning to tell my sister so they could prepare for the days to come. When I broke the good news, she was ecstatic. But at the same time, she became sad. Her husband and her oldest son were about to leave her.

I got back to the boat the same day. The boat crew was now standing by. Especially as a mechanic, I always wanted to know what else I could do to be better prepared. We were all very anxious for the next several days.

The day came. One of the owners came to the boat and let the captain and me know the day and time of action, which was in only three more nights. He told me to go back to Vung Tau and tell my brother-in-law to get ready and come to the location the day before. I went home the next day and relayed the message to my sister.

I also wanted to see my girlfriend; just in case this was the last time I would see her. I met her at our usual spot on the beach. It was a little windy that night. We felt a chill, so I held her in my arms the whole time. I closed my eyes and squeezed her body tightly into mine and I said to myself, *my love, somehow I feel strongly that I will leave you very soon.*

We ended the night as we saw the ocean was getting more violent; the wind was blowing strongly, and the big waves crashed onto the beach very hard. I gave her a very big kiss and a big hug. I told her to take good care of herself.

I said good-bye to my sister and her family the next morning, wishing my brother-in-law luck and saying I would see him and his son on the boat soon.

When I arrived at the boat, I could sense a different atmosphere at the fishing village. I met my boat crew, and the crew was happy to see me back. The captain told me we had to go fishing tonight. It was one night before we would set our plan into action.

Another day had passed, and tonight was the night. I believed that my brother-in-law and my nephew had already arrived at the designated location. In only several hours, the sky would turn dark, signaling the time for action. The sun was about to set. One of the owners came to the boat and shook each of our hands. Then the captain gave me the order, *"Let's start the engine."*

I started the engine, and the boat drifted away from the fishing village that I had become so familiar to me over the last several months. Soon, we came to the open water, and the sky was very dark. We put the fishing net down and pretended to fish for a little while. At the same time, I kept looking and monitoring the running of the engine. I worried, too much perhaps, and paid constant attention to the engine; but my engine kept running like a charm. I knew I loved my engine.

It was approaching the set time; we moved to the smaller canal and started searching for signals. Before long, we found several lights from smaller boats. We immediately got the boats side by side so we could load fuel, water, and food. It took us about half an hour to finish loading. Everything went according to the plan so far. People from the smaller boats told us the escapees would come aboard very soon. We all patiently waited.

Thirty minutes passed. We started to see more light signals heading our way. *"This is it!"* I screamed to the captain. I got more excited than ever. Before long, many smaller boats were approaching; then I started to hear the noise of people. Very soon, many people surrounded the big boat, trying to get on board. The situation became chaos. People were calling and yelling to each other without any organization. They were all very anxious to get on board as quickly as they could, and that made it a huge, disordered crown. The boat almost lost balance and capsized a few times. The situation made me extremely nervous.

At the same time, I was looking for my brother-in-law and my nephew. I started to call my brother-in-law's name, hoping that he would hear and respond back to me. I thought to myself that, if my brother and nephew didn't make it on the boat, I would get very upset and jump off the boat. Fortunately, I heard my brother's response, and now I knew his son and he were present in the crowd and then they made it on the boat safely.

The chaotic situation continued for at least thirty minutes. I thought that was one of my worst nightmares. Finally, I heard a strong voice from one of the owners. *"Let's get quiet and settled down; we need to get moving quickly before we get shot by the Vietcong."*

That put everyone in place and calmed people down. Soon the captain addressed everyone. *"We are now heading to the open sea."*

The boat was somewhat in order now. All the people were sitting in the various underneath compartments so that nobody would see any escapees on the boat. It was about five o'clock in the morning. The sky became brighter and brighter as the boat moved farther away from the shore.

The sun's lights appeared on the horizon. The people were sitting and relaxing after a few hours of horror at boarding time. It was also time for me to take a deep breath. Then a rush of thoughts sunk into my brain. Wow! I was actually escaping the Communists at last. I looked back to the shore. There was the cap of Vung Tau Island. It looked smaller and smaller, and then it disappeared as the boat kept floating away.

My feelings became very heavyhearted. My soul was crying; my heart was being broken. *Oh my God! I am actually leaving my country, my parents, and my family.* The pain of sorrow filled my stomach. I called out to my mother and my father.

I didn't know when I would be able to see them again, if ever. It was so painful that I just wanted to turn the boat around and go back home. I asked myself why I was suffering so much. Then I thought of my girlfriend. *My love! Don't you know that I am really leaving you?* My thoughts turned to my brother-in-law and my nephew. The husband was leaving the wife, who stayed home with four children. My nephew, who was just a young child had to leave his mother. The pain was so great; I thought I couldn't bear it.

Suddenly, we saw a vessel in the distance. We suspected it might be a Vietcong ship. That really woke me up and made me alert. The captain immediately steered our boat in the other direction. Fortunately, nothing happened, and we continued on the course. The weather was nice, and the sea was calm on the first day. My engine still kept singing the regular song. I never got bored but loved it. I prayed my engine would keep singing beautifully throughout the journey, no matter when we might see the land of freedom.

The sun was down, and the sky started getting dark. We were going to spend our first night on the high sea. I looked up, and I only saw the blank sky and massive water of Mother Nature around us. We were on the only boat that was floating in the space of emptiness. It was a very scary setting, even though the ocean was calm and no storm that we could predict loomed. At this time, we thought we had passed the patrolling barrier of the Communist. We were not really worrying about getting caught by the Vietcong anymore. We just worried about Mother Nature--her weather and her ocean.

When I had started working on this boat, I'd thought the boat was big and that I would feel safe, but my feeling now was totally opposite. This boat became very tiny, like a grain of sand in a desert, when we were floating in the deep sea. Our watercraft seemed like nothing; it looked like a little, dried leaf, drifting on the surface of an endless, vast body of water. As the sky got darker, the atmosphere got scarier. The majority of the people had never traveled on a fishing boat before, so many of them became very frightened. Also, many were Catholic, and they prayed together for the boat's safety. As the boat ran in the darkness, the chanting sound of the prayer that cried to God to have mercy on us and keep us safe made me feel like we were just about to die.

We had made it through the first night. I had barely gotten any sleep. The whole night, I had kept looking and listening to the engine running. I was so thankful that the engine had been running smoothly for the whole day. The darkness of the night started getting lighter as the morning arose. I saw the sun's lights shining from the East as it marked the beginning of our second day on the high seas. Everyone in the boat was tired but still in good spirits. However, many people began to question when we would see the new land.

Normally, as we'd often heard, it would take two to three days for the escaping boat to reach Malaysia if it had taken the right direction at a good speed. We also often heard that many refugee boats were rescued and picked up by American warships, such as the American Navy's Seventh Fleet, or any international cargo ships. Now we were in the second day, and we believed we should be in international water. We began scouting for the American aircraft carrier or any noncommunist cargo ship that might rescue us.

Some of us started asking a man—we called him the pilot of the boat—the prospects of the escaping route. He told us it would take us three to four days under his supervision for direction. The man claimed that he was a South Vietnamese Navy officer and knew a lot about sea navigation and compasses. He and his family were exempted from paying to escape. The boat owners hired him so he could lead the boat to the free land quickly and safely, and he aimed at Malaysia as our ultimate destination.

By the afternoon of the second day, my engine was still doing its job, and most of the men, women, and children were still doing well, some became very seasick, even though the ocean was fairly calm.

Suddenly, a dark cloud appeared on the horizon in the late afternoon; then we began to see big waves and choppy water, and there came the strong wind and rain. *Oh my God, please help us*, I prayed.

The condition of the sea was getting worse. Most people started getting sick and vomiting. Others began to cry. I felt a little seasick myself. I asked my brother-in-law to get me some soup so I would have something in my stomach. I knew that I couldn't get sick because I needed to take care of the engine. I tried to hold my own, keep spiritually and physically calm and feeling decent at all times. I had made it this far, and I knew I couldn't give up.

As the boat floating throughout the night, I continued to see the boat's struggle with the huge waves of the angry sea. Now I could really see the helplessness of our tiny boat. It was like thousands of pounds hung on a small string. The tiny boat could capsize easily if it couldn't fight the huge ten- to fifteen-foot waves. It looked like we all were about to die, so people continued praying, chanting, and asking the Lord for mercy.

Many times the boat struggled so hard against the strenuousness and violence of the unforgiving sea that I thought the huge waves were about to swallow the tiny boat completely. As a result, tremendous amounts of water rushed in both sides of the boat violently, and every time it happened, people screamed and cried even louder, terrorizing me with thoughts of imminent death.

I was at the back of the boat looking down at the engine. My entire body was soaking wet and cold every time the water rushed in. Water in the bottom of the boat had reached a very high level. This greatly increased the danger; the boat already carried so many people, and the extra water weight would make it more difficult for the boat to stay afloat as it battled the huge waves.

Despite our own fear, and the unbearable smell of the vomit from the passengers, my two assistants and I immediately jumped into the engine room. I asked my assistants to help me pump the water out. I had made two additional water pumps to prepare just for the time like this, and now I needed to use them. With the help of my friends, I got the water pump hooked up quickly and I made it run. What a difference it made. I was so happy to see the full force of pressure from the pipe pouring so much water out of the boat. I pumped all the water out only in fifteen to twenty minutes and made the boat light again.

However, as the captain kept fighting with the stormy weather throughout the night, more and more water continued to rush into both sides of the boat. My assistant and I had to stay put in the engine room and we had the water pumped out of the boat throughout the night.

We survived the night; the boat was still floating; my engine was still running, and the people stopped praying because they were all very sick and tired. The morning came, and the weather was somewhat improved but not calm. I was so exhausted that I had to lie down and get some sleep for a few hours. The choppy water made the boat run very bumpy.

When I woke up, it was still morning. I felt somewhat better after I had closed my eyes for a little while. Now we were on our third day at sea. I looked around, and I still saw only water around me. We all started expecting that we would be close to land. The food, water, and even fuel supply were three-fourths empty. We all grew concerned about the fate of our journey. We certainly didn't want to get lost at sea and end up with no destination. If that were to happen, our chances of survival would be very slim. We asked the pilot if he knew where we were and how much longer it would be before we could see land. He responded with a diffident tone that we might see the land of Malaysia in a day.

We continued going along the route that the pilot told the captain to take. The weather was still not cooperating; the skies remained very cloudy and the wind still strong. The condition of the high sea was still very rough. Sometimes, we got heavy rains. My brother-in-law, along with some others, tried to catch and save the water from the rains, suspecting that we might need it later on.

The evening of the third day had come, and another scary night was ahead of us. The waves were not as huge and the high sea was not as violent as the previous night, and the seawater didn't rush into the boat as often. But the horror of the dark had the same intensity. Most of the men and women squeezed the last ounce of their energy and poured it into praying and chanting again as the night fell. I closed my eyes and kneeled down in the back of the boat above the engine. I spoke to God and asked the Lord to save us, especially, since we had many women and children on board.

We made it through another night. The morning of the fourth day was here but the condition of the sea wasn't any different than yesterday. The sky was still very dark and no sunlight. The only thing that could bring a very weak smile to my face was that I saw many dolphins were swimming and playfully jumping up and down alongside our running boat. I thought that the dolphins were communicating with us. Perhaps they were trying to cheer up the people on the boat and give us a positive feeling, a message that we shouldn't be worry; we would be all right and we would find the land of freedom. Or maybe the dolphins were signaling that help would be on the way. I went to the side of the boat and reached my hand down, trying to touch the dolphins. These were beautiful and smart sea creatures and I wanted to talk to them desperately. *"Hey, dolphins, could you please show me the best and shortest way to land?"* My words only disappeared into the sea spray.

By midday, we were still in the middle of nowhere in the ocean. We saw no land and no American or international ship. We saw nothing but water. The food, water, and fuel supply were running very low now. I could see the exhaustion and desperation on everyone's face. Many of us turned to the pilot of the boat and asked him again about the fate of our journey. Once again, his answer was that it might take another day. We believed that the pilot was nobody. He made up all the stories about his experience and knowledge about sea navigation so he could get away without paying for his family's escape. In fact, we found out that he had brought with him a sea compass, the most crucial piece of equipment for navigation, was broken and no good to use. That was very discouraging news for all the escapees, and we wondered if we had been lost in the high seas. Would we ever make it to Malaysia or any land? Or would we all eventually become food for fish in the deep ocean?

The sky was getting dark, the night almost upon us, and the fourth day of the journey almost over, but the desperate boat was still floating somewhere in the ocean. Oh my God! When would we see the light at the end of the tunnel? The only thing that warmed my heart now was my engine. It had been running all of these days continuously without a single problem. I loved it so much for being so good to me. Without the engine running and the water pumps working, we would all be drowned already. But realizing that nobody knew when we would reach the free land really saddened my heart. There was so much sorrow and hurt deep within my soul. I looked up at the dark sky and cried to God for help. I also called out to my mother and father. *"Don't you know your son and grandson might die in the middle of the ocean?"*

In the morning, I thanked God we had made it through another scary night. On the fifth day of the journey, we were still experiencing strong winds and huge waves. Nothing had really changed as far as the condition of the high sea. Nevertheless, the water and food supply was almost completely gone. We only had some of the fuel left, possibly enough to keep my engine going for one more day.

I was fatigued from many nights without sleep. Even so, I was still walking and talking and taking care of my engine. Perhaps God had given me the energy to stay put so I could do the things I needed to do to help the tiny boat stay afloat. I looked at the captain, and I asked how he was doing. He seemed to have more energy than the rest of the crew. As I understood, he had been a fisherman for a number of years. He was definitely the right man for the job.

I admired and respected him for all his hard work and his skill. Many times, he'd had to tie his foot to the steering stick because the strong waves slamming into the boat threatened to cause him to lose steering leverage. If he lost the leverage of the steer, the boat could be easily capsized by the huge waves.

Most of the people on the boat were very drained and had no more energy left. I clearly saw the hopelessness on their faces. All we could do now was to pray to God to lead the way. Our fate was totally in God's hands.

Half of the fifth day had passed, and we still saw nothing. We kept scouting for some sign that would point us in the right direction—a direction that would lead to land; the hope only turned into hopelessness. I got so tired of looking to the distance then I turned my full attention to my engine. Seeing my engine continue to run smoothly and efficiently all these days was the only thing that gave me energy. I didn't know whether we would make it to land, but I knew I had done what I needed to do, and I was very satisfied with myself. As long as the engine kept running, I believed the escapees still had a slim chance to make it to land; if the engine stopped running, the whole journey would stand still, and everyone's life would definitely be in serious danger.

The boat kept moving through the very rough weather. I wished the sea were calm with a sunny, clear sky that would boost up our spirits. Instead, the boat still stumbled against the big waves. I looked at several faces, and I saw nothing left in them. The beginnings of dying human flesh were clearly in the corners of my fellow passengers' eyes. I put my head down, sorrow and dolefulness flooding into me. Why had my people suffered so much? If there were freedom and justice in our fatherland, we would not have gone through this dreadful journey. The Communists of Vietnam ultimately terrorized their own people in many different ways and they should be responsible for million of deaths of the people of Vietnam.

I suddenly noticed tears were in my eyes. *I shouldn't cry!* I reminded myself. I stood up and wiped my tears away. I told myself that I was not afraid to die. If I died, I knew I would die for my own beliefs, just like millions of Vietnamese who had been terrorized and killed by the Vietnamese Communist regime.

Just as I stood up with that strong thought in my mind, I looked out, and in the far distance, I saw a small, black dot appear in the middle of the water. I screamed from the top of my lungs *"Oh my God! I see an island."*

Then I looked at my people and screamed again, *"My people! We see an island ahead of us."*

I was ecstatic. And only minutes later, the dot was getting larger and larger.

"We make it to land," somebody else shouted.

But as we got closer, I saw what we were really looking at. *"Oh my God!"* I shouted. *"It's a big ship!"*

The ship was also heading in our direction and that was why we saw it so quickly.

As soon as we'd identified the big ship, the captain and other people on the boat shot flairs in the sky to signal that we were in distress. We also raised the SOS flag to let the big ship know that we needed to be rescued. Then we prayed that the ship would rescue us. As we came close to the ship, it slowed and then stopped. We all became very excited. *"The ship sees us,"* someone screamed. *"They will rescue us!"* someone else joined in.

The Cap Anamur, my supreme angel on the Pacific Ocean.

Our boat got closer and closer and—wow!—the ship was huge. I had never before seen a ship that huge. Our boat looked like a grasshopper next to an 18-wheeler truck. We saw the name of the ship—*Cap Anamur.* We had no idea what kind of ship it was or what country it belonged to. Then we looked up to the ship deck and saw a man with a loudspeaker in his hand. He spoke down to us in Vietnamese saying that we needed to be calm so the ship could start the process of rescuing us. Somebody spoke in Vietnamese! I wondered and questioned that was this a Vietnamese Communists ship?

Now in order to start the rescue, our boat had to stop, but stopping the tiny boat in the rough sea could be so dangerous. I saw the people on the ship put down a large rope ladder along the side of the ship so we could climb up. The ship also lowered a crane that hooked to a large net to pick up children and women who could not climb up the rope ladder.

The process was very challenging and risky, but with hard work, the skill of our captain, and the ship's equipment, we were all rescued in only a few hours.

I was one of the last people to be rescued. I still needed to hang on with the captain and ensure that the engine remained running as the captain maneuvered the boat during the rescue process. When I climbed up on that rope and took my very first step on the ship, I knew that I was saved—that I had stayed alive, along with my people on the boat. I looked up in the sky and now I knew God had been watching us. *Thank you, Lord. We were just about to die and you directed the ship to come and save us.*

I could not describe my feeling when I first stepped onto that ship. The ship had saved our bodies and our souls. I looked down to my boat and I could see how tiny the boat was. I could not believe we had survived in that small vessel through the deep ocean. I said good-bye to my boat

My boat at the time of our rescue by Cap Anamur.

and the engine I loved. The boat was my angel, and the engine was my heart and soul. I whispered to the boat, *"I took care of you so well, and you in turn took care of all the people on the boat. Thank you! You served our purpose—the purpose of life, the purpose of humanity."*

Interestingly, when I stepped on the ship, barely able to walk, I saw many other Vietnamese on the ship. I couldn't understand how the ship had so many Vietnamese people on board. I was confused and a little scared; I thought that this might be a Vietcong ship. But I saw that the captain of the ship and he didn't look like a Vietnamese. Then I met a translator who was Vietnamese, Huan. Huan spoke to me and told me that *Cap Anamur* was a German ship, which was sponsored and supported by the West German government with the sole mission of rescuing the dying Vietnamese boat people along the coast of south and middle of Vietnam.

Huan was also a boat people himself who had been rescued a few years ago by the same ship, and now he wanted to volunteer with the *Cap Anamur* to help his own people. He was instrumental in the ship's rescue missions. The first voice spoken down to our boat in Vietnamese, that I wondered, was Huan's voice. This really blew me away. I thought I was dreaming. I couldn't believe that such a ship patrolled the Pacific Ocean, hunted boat people who desperately needed to be rescued.

Furthermore, I learned that this ship had rescued thousands of boat people and saved thousands of human souls. The ship had become the supreme angel watching over the Vietnamese boat people in the Pacific Ocean.

The captain of our boat did a head count—one hundred and one people from my tiny boat; everyone had been saved. We got together on the big ship and celebrated our survival. We hugged and touched one another, knowing that we were safe and alive. Some of us wept for joy. What a happy moment it was. We were free at last, and no words could describe our feelings. The ship's crew gave us clean clothing and food. Huan took all of us to a big room, where beds were ready for us to rest and recuperate. I was still thinking that I was living in a dream.

My brother-in-law got help as he climbed up to the Cap Anamur.

The time now was very late in the afternoon. By the time I got cleaned up and had some food, it was nighttime. I was looking forward to lying down and resting. I checked with my brother-in-law and my nephew, whose bed was next to mine. I grasped my nephew in my arms and squeezed his body really tight and I told him that we had made it. I said good night to my brother-in-law and my nephew and then went to sleep.

I suddenly woke up just a few hours later. The ship was rocking very badly. I learned that the ship was now passing through a very serious storm. I got goose bumps all over my skin and realized that if this big ship was rocking, this must be a very bad storm. Oh my Lord! This proved it that God had watched over us. If we hadn't been rescued several hours ago, we would not have survived the journey. I was 100 percent certain that my tiny boat couldn't make it through this storm; we would have been capsized in the middle of night and everyone would have drowned. The Lord had definitely saved us. I closed my eyes again and said to the Lord, *Thank you.*

I shut my eyes again and I slept the whole night through. I got up in the morning, and I had never felt better. Now I no longer had to worry about my safety. I felt so light for being not stressed out about the functioning of my boat engine anymore. I had seen the light at the end of the tunnel, and I felt very lucky to be well and alive. Everyone else also looked decent after facing the extreme danger of the journey. We all thought that we were going to die. I was so grateful for the entire boat people were safe and sound.

VIII

I settled into living on the ship. Now that I didn't have to worry about my survival, all my feeling and thoughts went to my country and my family. I couldn't believe I finally, actually, and successfully had made the escape and I couldn't believe this was real. I had physically left my country, but my feeling hadn't kicked in and fully realized that yet. Many nights I would wake up on the ship not fully aware of where I was because I was still dreaming. Then when I was wide-awake, I would ask myself when I would ever return to my country. My heart also saddened thinking of my family. I wished I could let my parents and my sister know that we had made it to safety and we were well and alive. My heart broke when I realized that I didn't know when I would ever see them again. I also thought of my girlfriend whom I'd left behind. She didn't know what I had gone out of the country and that I had almost died in the ocean. I would be missing her dearly for many days to come.

The ship continued its search and rescue mission. Only a few days after my boat was rescued, I witnessed a rescue from the ship myself. It was another afternoon with a rough sea; the ship had intercepted a refugee boat in distress. I stood a short distance from the rescue operation area, and I thought I was watching a movie. I saw the boat, which was very similar to my boat, except it was a little larger. There were also more people on this boat. I was so happy to see them get rescued. I wished I could hug each and every one of them and congratulate them right at that time for successfully escaping from the Communist regime. Once again, the supreme angel *Cap Anamur* had saved another group of Vietnamese boat people.

The *Cap Anamur* continued searching for the desperate boat people. Day after day, I went to the top of the ship and hoped to see another rescue. Several days passed, and I hadn't seen another boat. I figured that the country coastline was thousands of miles and the water was vast and endless. How could the ship intercept a refugee boat in the big Pacific Ocean like this? The chances for the boat people to be rescued were very slim. The truth sunk in--thousands of Vietnamese boat people had surely died in the deep ocean without anyone ever knowing their fate. I was one of the luckiest persons on this earth to be alive.

I was floating with the ship for a few weeks. The ship eventually took all the boat people to Palawan, an island province of the Philippines. A refugee camp set up and supported by the International Refugee Committee awaited us. I couldn't wait to see land again. This time, the land that I was going to see wasn't just any land. This land would be the land of the free, even though I knew were just going to a refugee camp. This would be the first time I would step on free land since the Fall of Saigon in 1975.

My supreme angel arrived at the Palawan Port.

Also, when I got to land, I needed to find ways to communicate and let my family know we were alive and had made it to the Philippines. At the same time, I needed to get in touch with my first brother, who lived in Green Bay, Wisconsin, at the time. I was certain that, when he got the news, it would blow him away.

The ship arrived at the port very late in the afternoon one day in July 1981. A heavy rain fell as we got off the ship and boarded a bus that took us to the refugee camp. Now it was very dark, and the heavy rain made settling down that first evening in the camp very rough. The camp organizer people welcomed us by giving us some canned food and blankets. We just lay down on the floor for the first night of sleep in the camp.

IX

$\mathscr{T}$omorrow I would obtain my identification and officially become a refugee. The refugee camp was very simple and made up of temporary housing. It contained about three to four thousand Vietnamese boat people at this time. Most of the refugees had arrived by boats that had come straight from Vietnam to the shores of the Philippines. The rest were boat people who had been rescued by *Cap Anamur* or American warships or, to a smaller degree, other international ships.

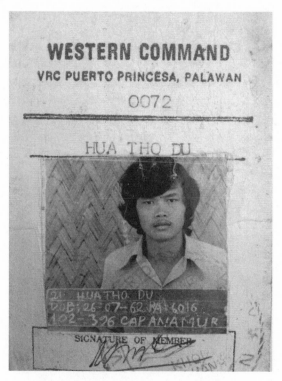

My identification at the Vietnamese Refugee Center.

I am writing letters to my sister.

I knew that the road ahead of me would be bumpy. People living here depended on the basic food supply from the camp day per day. Most of the shelters had been constructed from small pieces of wood and long grasses from the nearby jungle. People here tried to make daily living as best they could, although the living here was not proper compared to the lowest standard of living, especially when it came to toiletry, sanitation, and running water. Electricity and running water were extremely limited. We were only allowed one light bulb for each housing structure.

My friends and I at the flower garden center of the RPC.

But one thing was sure—nothing could stop the people from living freely and happily outside the Communists of Vietnam. We had found lives through struggle, brutalization, and death. We all realized that this was a temporary stay, while we awaited settlement in a third country. For me, I was more eager than ever for the day I could reunite with my brother in the United States of America.

For the next several days, my brother-in-law and I tried to send letters to family in Vietnam, letting them know that we had made it to the Philippines. I also contacted my brother in the United States through collect calls. I couldn't believe I was hearing his voice for the first time after almost seven years of separation. I told him to start the sponsorship paperwork so I could reunite with him as soon as possible. I also told him that my brother-in-law and my nephew and I needed some money so we could make our lives here in the refugee camp a bit easier.

In only a few weeks, I got an interview when the American Embassy came to the camp. The interviewers asked me why I wanted to settle in the United States. I responded that I had a blood brother who was living in the United States and I just needed to reunite with him. They listened to my reason and said they would let me know whether I would be accepted to go to America. All I needed to do now was to be patient and wait for the news—good news hopefully.

While living here, I had to start thinking about my new life and new directions. The most important thing for me now was to learn to speak the English language. I registered in some Basic English classes that were given by our own boat people in the camp. I loved learning; I always wanted to prepare for what was coming. At this time, I was eighteen years of age, and learning a new language at that age wasn't that easy. My brother-in-law and I also volunteered in some organizations of the camp. I joined to help in a small refugee clinic that took care of some of the common illnesses of the boat people contracted from living in the camp.

The first period of living in the camp was very tough. I was really homesick. I missed my country and my family so much. I wanted to go to Palawan Beach every evening so I could watch the sunset. The sunsets here were similar to those in Vietnam. Its beautiful scene of the sun at the end of the sky and its reflection in the blue water blending the colorful clouds from above stretching out on the horizon created a beautiful picture just before the sun's disappearing. This picture was what I saw in my country. I wished I were a bird so I could fly to the other side of the ocean and see my beautiful country once again. I wondered how my parents were doing. Did the Vietcong give them a hard time when they knew their son had escaped the regime? What about my sister and brother who were still there under the Vietcong regulations? I really wished they were all here with me. Many nights, the camp broadcasted through loudspeakers many patriotic songs about the love of my country and my people. That tore up my heart. I missed my country tremendously.

I also thought of my girlfriend. I missed her dearly, and I was sure she lived there miserably without seeing me. I sent her several letters telling her I was willing to wait for her if she would try to escape the country. She understood, and she told me in her letter she would try. I couldn't imagine how much she would mean to me if I had her here with me.

Several weeks had passed, and everyone in the camp was anxiously awaiting good news from his or her third country settlement. I was no different. One day, the mail office called out the names of people who had mail. My name was called twice, which indicated that I should have two letters. I immediately ran to the mail office and stood in line to receive my mail. I couldn't wait to see the mails. I hoped to receive the acceptance letter from the American Embassy. When it was my turn to be served, the mailman gave me two letters. Indeed, one letter was from the American Embassy, and the other was from my girlfriend.

I was so happy that the embassy had responded to me already. I stepped aside and immediately opened the envelope. Surprisingly, I expected the worst news. The American Embassy had denied my request to reunite with my brother. They asked me to go to Germany because a German ship had rescued me. My heart froze. I asked myself why the US officials didn't want me to come and live with my own brother in the States. I just couldn't understand.

Then I opened my girlfriend's letter. I saw the familiar handwriting, and I was ready to absorb all of her emotions. I had been waiting for her letter because I had sent her several letters already. I missed her so much, and I couldn't wait to read her letter, even though I knew it would be nothing but sadness. Oh my God! Her letter broke my heart into pieces. I couldn't finish reading the letter at first because it was too much for me to bear. She was miserable and suffering the love that she missed. I finished reading it without realizing that tears—the tears of losing my first true love—were on my eyes. She mentioned in the letter that the last time we met at the Vung Tau beach, she had sensed that she was going to lose me. I felt so much pain reading each and every word in her letter. All I could do now was put her letter on my chest against my heart and let my soul cry, "*I am so sorry.*"

When sad news came, it usually never came once but many times at the same time. That was what had happened to me. The American Embassy had rejected me, and my girlfriend's letter told me that she was totally miserable when she realized that I had left the country. I felt so many guilds and it was very difficult for me not to fall into utter depression. I needed to stand up and face the reality. Why had the American Embassy rejected my request? Who wouldn't want to reunite with his or her family members, especially when living in a foreign country? He was my oldest brother, and I loved him dearly despite all those years of separation. I felt strongly that I needed to fight. This was my life. Nothing came easily and readily for me. I had always had to struggle and combat. This was no different. I determined to appeal the American Embassy and resubmit my request. I wanted to let them know that I wouldn't settle for what they had done to me.

X

$\mathscr{I}$had been living in the camp for three months now and the life here was getting rougher. More and more refugees had arrived at the camp—flooded waves of boat people escaping from Vietnam.

One time, the camp welcomed a small group of refugees. This group's story horrified everyone in the camp. Their boat had been floating in the Pacific Ocean for several weeks. The boat's engine had totally broken down and they'd had no water or food supply for such a very long period of time. Their helpless bodies just lay on the boat that was drifting in whatever direction the sea current or wind took it. They became so starved and thirsty that many of them couldn't hang on; they drank the seawater and became more dehydrated and died. The survivors told us that they had dropped the first few dead bodies into the ocean, but they had had to eat the human flesh from the next wave of the dead persons and use their urine as water to stay alive. Their boat finally drifted to a Filipino island. The group was eventually transferred to this refugee camp. What a story! I really cried for my people. The survivals of this boat looked like moving skeletons—barely alive.

The wave of the boat people riding the Southeast Asian Sea continued on a large scale. I was very happy to see that so many of us had successfully escaped the Communist regime; but this small camp had become very concentrated. Several thousand refugees now lived in the camp. All of us who had stayed in the camp for some time wished to leave the camp to make room for the newcomers.

I had my own problem; I guessed I would have to stay here a lot longer if I decided to fight with the American Embassy. I waited patiently for a few weeks until the American Embassy came to visit again. I had to resubmit the paperwork, along with the notice of disagreement about their denial of my previous application. I also told them humbly that I would go to Germany with no hesitation because Germany was also a great, free country, except that my own brother was living in the United States. The embassy officials accepted my second application, and I hoped I had made my case. I prayed they would give me a second chance.

I really missed my brother dearly. He was eleven years older than me, but I still had many fond memories with him when I was just a small boy. He used to bring many of his friends home, and they all made fun of his little, youngest brother. I also remembered him awarding me a lot of money when I was the best student in my school. It would be so great for me to see him again and my parents would be extremely happy. I couldn't wait for that dream to come true. I hoped I was almost there. I had just one more step—the approval of the American Embassy.

Months passed, and one day, I received the second letter from the American Embassy. Guess what? The embassy had denied me again. I wanted to break down and weep. I was utterly brokenhearted, and I didn't know what to do. I wanted to scream loudly and demand to know why this was happening to me. I hadn't done anything wrong, and I hadn't asked anything unreasonable. Why did I have to go through this? It was a huge frustration and desperation for me.

I held the letter in my hand, and I showed it to my brother-in-law. I told him that I was very disappointed and upset. He suggested that he and I should take a taxi to the nearby city, where we could call my brother in the States and ask him why this was happening.

Fortunately, my brother was home, and he answered the call. He was very surprised and upset, too. He told me I should not give up. Just be patient and find a way to submit a third request, he advised. At the same time, he would double-check with his sponsor agency in the States and find out what he needed to do to correct the process. My brother finally calmed me down, and I followed his advice.

Another few weeks passed while I waited for the American Embassy to visit again. When the embassy officials came, I requested to see them. I turned in my application for the third time. Before leaving the office, I told them again that I really needed to go to the States with my brother. I also told them that I hoped they would reprocess and accept my application. They took my application, and I just prayed I wouldn't have to go through this again.

I tried to live the normal days in the refugee camp. Too much worrying would only bring down my spirit. After all, I had successfully escaped and

I was alive. I didn't have to live with the Vietcong anymore. So if I had to stay here a little longer for the reconciliation the settlement with the American Embassy was okay with me. Every time there was a denial meant two to three months delay. I knew that eventually I would have a place to go. Anything would be better than living with the Communists. Now I might use this time to learn English. I would keep trying to occupy myself and do something good and productive while waiting. I had been in the refugee for five months, and I just had to take it one day at a time.

Life in the camp on the island became more difficult because it was so concentrated, but it was also fun sometimes. I loved to go to the beach and play with my nephew. He was a stubborn little boy, but we had a good time together.

Several weeks had passed since I'd turned in my application for the third time. Every day I checked my mail carefully, and one day, indeed, I received a letter from the American Embassy. I opened the letter immediately and I was informed that I had been accepted to settle in the United States of America.

God had answered my prayer. I was extremely happy. All of my patience and determination had paid off. Now I could close the chapter of waiting for the American Embassy to accept me. I wanted to scream out loud, *Thank you, Lord. Thank you, America.*

My nephew, friends, and me at the Palawan Beach.

All people who were going to the States had to go to five to six months of language and orientation session on a different island of the Philippines called Bataan. It wasn't too long before I noticed my name on the manifest of the refugees who were going to transfer to Bataan. I knew that I would have to leave behind my brother-in-law and my nephew in the Palawan Island very soon. They had to stay in here and wait for a short while for their settlement in West Germany. I also thought of many good friends with whom I'd shared all the tough times in this refugee camp. So much emotion went through my mind.

The time had come for my departure to Bataan. It was a cloudy day. My brother-in-law and nephew, along with a group of my friends, took the bus to the seaport so they could see leaving the island. I was happy that I was in the process of transferring for my orientation course—it marked the change for the better in my life—but it was a heavyhearted day. Saying good-bye to many friends and especially to my nephew, who was just six year of age, was difficult.

The horn of the ferry ship sounded; I had to board. The ship started moving, and I stood in the back of the ship and waved good-bye to my friends until I could no longer see them.

The huge ferryboat took many refugees to new camps.

The ship arrived at Bataan before that evening. The buses were already there waiting, and they took us to the new refugee camp before nightfall. This was a much better refugee camp with better structures. I was assigned to live in a small apartment with other refugees. I settled in for the night; tomorrow I would find out about my orientation classes. I couldn't wait to start my classes. I was eager to learn the new language and the culture of the United States of America.

The day my friends saw me transfer to a new refugee camp.

Here I was in a new environment and atmosphere. I met several friends from Palawan, and they were here for the same purpose. I was very excited for the first day of my formal English class. The teacher was Pilipina, and I really liked her. She was very energetic and motivating. I knew that learning the new language in an adult was going to be very challenging. But I had no choice if I wanted to have good communication skills. I wanted not only that but to go farther and beyond. I wanted to become a good citizen of the new country that was going to harbor me. I wanted to have a good career and be able to demonstrate my responsibility. I wanted to help and serve other citizens, just as the people of the United States were helping me at this time. Without the funding and support of the people of the United State of America, I wouldn't be here in a good classroom learning English. Without America promoting and protecting freedom and liberty around the world, I wouldn't be free and probably would have been killed in a Communist prison. I was so thankful for the precious freedom.

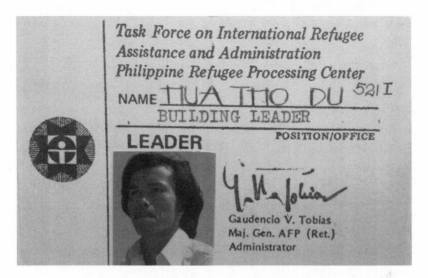

Task Force on International Refugee
Assistance and Administration
Philippine Refugee Processing Center
NAME HUA THO DU 521 I
BUILDING LEADER
LEADER   POSITION/OFFICE

Gaudencio V. Tobias
Maj. Gen. AFP (Ret.)
Administrator

I served as a building leader when staying in the camp.

After a few months, I had finished the first session of English class. It was time for me to enroll in the orientation class. Then I would be on my way to America. The second half of the program taught refugees how to find jobs, rent an apartment, shop for food or clothing, and so on. There was too much to learn in such a short period. I hoped I would retain all of my learning when I arrived in the United States.

The final session of my English class with my Filipino teacher.

Time flew quickly. Four months had passed already, and I graduated from the orientation class. The only thing left for me to do was to wait for my name to appear on the manifest to fly to America. My dream was just about to come true. I was excited about everything. The prospect of being a truly free man living in a country with freedom and dignity dominated my thoughts. It would be so awesome to see my big brother, who I had not seen for a very long period of time and I thought I would never be able to see him again.

Next, I would wonder what America looked like. I had heard so many wonderful things about the United States of America, and I was thrilled to see this great country with my own eyes. Furthermore, I had been told that America was the land of opportunity. I knew that I would work very hard to make opportunities so I could become productive citizen so I could serve back to my new country.

And then one day, I saw my name on the manifest. That day in September 1982 was my big day—the day I had been waiting in my dream. My eighteen-month journey that had started with a life-and-death escape from the Communist regime and then the waiting for the settlement in two refugee camps would come to an end. I was twenty years old now, but I felt so good with the fresh to restart my life in the free and most powerful country on earth. I only had a few more days to get packed and be ready for the ultimate trip to freedom.

I couldn't sleep the night before because it was so much thinking in my mind. All good and bad memories kept circling in my head. I just couldn't believe I had made it this far. I thought I was still living in my dream and had never woken up. It was just too good to be true. Tomorrow I would start my trip to America. I tossed and turned for several hours in bed. I got so tired that, suddenly, my eyes and my brain shut down. I went into the deepest sleep.

But somehow I felt that I got lost and walking in a very wild jungle. I tried to find the way out to a civil setting but I couldn't and I was so scared. I called for my mother and my father loudly so they would come and help me, but no one showed up. Then I saw a small shadow of a person in a big bush from a distance. I ran toward the bush, screaming, *"Help! Help!"*

As I got a little closer, I saw a woman with a guerilla hat; her long hair fell passed her waist, and she was holding a big AK-47 in her arms. Oh my

God! She was one of the Vietcong. I started running away quickly, but I tripped and fell. The female guerilla came close to me when I was on the ground. I saw her reload her AK-47. Her eyes were fixed in an angry, evil face. She pointed the gun at me with her finger pulling the trigger.

"*No!*" I screamed. "*Don't shoot!*"

I sat up. Sweat covered my forehead. It was a just a horrible nightmare. I couldn't believe I still had bad dreams about the Vietcong up to the very last night I stayed in the refugee camp.

I had to get up, even though it was still very early. I didn't want to go to sleep any more. I took a shower, organized all my belongings and paperwork, and made myself a large cup of coffee. I sat down, relaxed, and looked beyond the green mountains of the Philippine Islands.

It was time for me to go. Several friends came by and walked with me to the bus. I said good-bye to my friends, and we promised to keep in touch. We hoped we would see each other in America. The bus started moving as I waved to my friends for the last time. The bus headed to the capital, Manila. We would stay there for a night; the bus would take us to Manila International Airport the next morning, and then we would board an airplane headed for America. I arrived in the transit camp in Manila in the evening after a few hours on the road.

I spent my last night in the Philippines in the transit camp. I counted every hour that passed. I hoped I could get some sleep tonight. I was so anxious and couldn't wait for the morning to come. Tomorrow was only several hours away, and it would be an exciting day. I knew that I would be like Bambi tomorrow because everything around me would be so new and I probably wouldn't know what to do or how to react. I couldn't imagine myself in a big airplane flying to America.

XI

Tomorrow was here. I woke up very early and got myself ready for the bus. I arrived at the Manila airport a few hours later. I couldn't believe what I saw. What a big airport it was; the airplanes were huge. My eyes opened wide to see everything that was surrounding me. My group just followed the guide. Before long, I was boarding the biggest airplane I'd ever seen. The airplane took off; I got so nervous but exciting when we became airborne. I'd never had that special feeling like that before. This was the first time I had ever flown in a jet airplane in my life. Fortunately, I didn't get airsick.

Several hours later, the airplane prepared for landing. It had to stop in Honolulu, Hawaii, for fuel. When the airplane was going down, I looked through the window, and I saw a spectacular view. The blue ocean surrounded the green of the forests of the beautiful island. The airplane was very close to the earth as it was approaching a huge city with tall, striking buildings, and traffic flowed on the beautiful freeways and streets in an orderly manner that made the city look so vibrant and alive. What a stunning scene it was. I told myself, *this is what free land looks like, and I am really seeing the beautiful lights at the end of the tunnel.*

The airplane was on the ground for more than thirty minutes. Then it took off again. This time, it was flying to San Francisco, California. It had to fly through the night and would arrive at the San Francisco Airport the next morning. It was a very long flight, but I just sat tight and enjoyed my flight and prayed to have a safe flight all the way. Many times I bowed my head and held my hands together and thanked to God who had allowed me to sit on this airplane. This was magical; I still couldn't believe that my dream was coming true. How could anyone believe that a very poor young man who might have been caught, killed, or brutalized many times by the Communists was now sitting in an airplane heading to the United States of America? I considered myself the luckiest person on earth.

The airplane was ready to land at the San Francisco Airport late the next morning. Here was another unbelievable, beautiful, and gigantic city I saw through the window. Then the airplane had landed, and I did all I could not to scream out loud because I was so excited. I told myself, *I am here; I have arrived on the mainland of the United States of America!*

I got off the airplane and walked through the gate. I saw the person holding a sign that directed all the refugees to follow her. We got all our belongings and followed her to a bus. I fell behind the group somehow, and I tried to catch up. I saw big glass doors in front of me several feet away; I put my belongings down so I could open the glass doors. But as I walked close, the doors automatically opened. I wondered how the doors had done that. Then I went back and got my belongings and headed to the doors; the doors were already closed. I just couldn't understand that. Once again, I put my stuff down and went toward the doors with my free hands. As I got close, the doors opened again. Why did the doors kept opening without anybody to open them? Then I saw people walking through, and I just followed them through the doors. After passing through the doors, I looked back and wondering about the magic glass doors.

I ran after them and tried to catch up. I finally got in pace with the group. We boarded the bus, and it took us to a transit center near the airport. The weather was chilly, and I felt very cold. We walked into a building, and several people were standing by big carton boxes. As we walked in, the people opened the box and handed us very nice, warm jackets. I couldn't believe it. Somebody really understood and prepared for what we would need. I didn't know what to say but simply thanked the person who gave me the jacket. I immediately put the jacket on, and it made me feel warm right away. They also handed out lunchboxes for the day.

I finally got to a room with a few other refugees. I knew that I had to stay here for the night. I took out my paperwork and looked for the flight ticket with the information for tomorrow's flight to Houston, Texas, my final destination. Tomorrow would also be another big day—one I had been dreaming about for years; it was the day I would see my brother and I couldn't wait.

Night started to fall on the big city. I wished I could go out and take a peek at the city in the nighttime. I was sure the city would be unbelievable. I really needed some rest tonight. I hadn't rested well lately. I got into the bed that was already made up with nice pillows and a thick, furry blanket. It was so nice to lie down and sleep on this little comfy bed.

I had just started to close my eyes to try and get some sleep but someone knocked on the door. I opened my eyes and looked to the door as a fellow refugee opened it. The guest appeared to be a service lady and she wanted to ask us if we were okay or needed anything. We thanked her and told her we were good and all set for the night.

Somebody really cared about us. That really affected me. I wondered who was behind all of these good deeds. I should realize that creating this organization and carrying out this mission of charity had required tremendous time, money, and effort. I wanted to say, *Thank you*. But words were definitely not enough. I knew those volunteers had to work very hard to care for all refugees every step of the way until we met our sponsors or family members. What they did was priceless, and I owed them my deepest gratitude.

I tried to sleep, but it was so hard. The different time zones had thrown me out of my natural rhythm. All I could do was close my eyes and put my mind at ease; but I couldn't even do that. Then a picture of my parents came to my mind. I wondered how they were doing and how their health was. They didn't know that I had made it to the United States of America and that tomorrow I would see their eldest son in Houston. That would be stunning news for them; they would be extremely happy and so proud of their sons. I missed them so dearly. I wished I could share all my feelings with them at this time. I prayed for all of my family at home. I continued tossing and turning on my bed underneath my comfortable and secure blanket.

The night was long, but it was finally over when I saw some early morning sunlight shining through my window. I woke up and got ready for my last trip. After breakfast, I went down to the waiting area for the bus. It arrived half an hour later. I boarded the bus along with many other refugees, and soon we were heading to the airport.

We were going to different terminals for many different destinations. I found out that two other refugees were also going to Houston, Texas. The three of us boarded together on the same airplane. I was so glad to have some company. We were all very excited and couldn't wait to see our family members.

The flight was just over three hours long. Before I knew it, the airplane was getting ready for landing. I looked down to the city—another spectacular view. It was different from San Francisco, though. I hoped my brother was there waiting to see me. I couldn't wait for the plane to land. I clapped my hands when we landed safely at the Houston International Airport. When the airplane stopped completely, I gathered all my belongings.

Once out of the airplane, I walked slowly through the first gate. I searched for my brother. Then I walked through a bigger gate where a lot of people were coming and going from many directions. I worried about how I would be able to find my brother in such a crowded area. I hoped that he would be able to recognize me. Once out of the gate, I made my way slowly forward.

Then I looked straight in front of me, and there he was! He was standing there with his wife and a few of his friends, and they were all waiting for me. I jumped toward him and gave him a big hug. What a moment it was. I felt numb because it was hard for me to acknowledge my dream becoming reality. I was hugging him as I was hardly saying his name in my throat. It was an incredibly happy ending with the happy tears—this reunion of two brothers who had been separated for so long by two different continents.

My brother introduced to me his wife, whom I had never met before, and he also introduced his friends. We then left the airport. I got into my brother's car, and he drove home to his apartment about forty minutes away.

Once again, I was starting another brand-new chapter of my life—the chapter of a refugee just starting his life in America.

XII

I wrote letters to my parents and told them that I had finally reunited with their eldest son in this great country. I also wrote to my girlfriend, telling her that I had just arrived and settled in the United States of America. I asked her never stop trying to escape so that I would keep the hope alive that, one day, I would see her here in America.

I stayed home for about a week, just relaxing and adapting to my new environment and routines. Everything here was totally new and different. I knew I had a very long road ahead of me.

One day at our family dinner, I started talking with my brother about going back to school. I told him that I didn't only need to learn English but I also needed to finish high school, which I hadn't had the chance to complete when I was in Vietnam.

I longed for all those days when I was learning and competing with my classmates in junior high school. I loved mathematics and science. I loved chemistry, biology, and physics. I was not the smartest student, but I loved to study hard and compete with my friends in a good way. I wanted to do that all over again, not in Vietnam but in my new country. It would be so amazing if I could do that in this great nation. I asked my brother if he could take me to a high school nearby and help me to enroll.

He did just that. He got a day off and took me to a local high school. We both walked into the admission office. At that time, I still barely spoke any English, so my brother did all the talking. He asked the lady in the office if he could register me. The lady asked my brother how old I was. My brother responded that I was twenty years of age. I saw the woman shake her head. She told my brother that I was over the age limit and she couldn't register me for the high school.

My face turned very long, and I was so disappointed as we were walking out of the admission office. On the way home, I asked him what I should do. My brother didn't answer me and stayed silent.

Days went by, and I struggled with thoughts of going back to school myself. I felt that a day I stayed home not learning was a day I wasted my brain. One day, a friend of my brother told me that she knew an English as a Second Language (ESL) evening program that was available to everyone. The classes were held in a church that was about a twenty-minute drive away. I thought that was a good start.

I asked my brother's friend if she could take me to the church and help me register for my ESL class the next day because my brother had to work. She said she was willing to help me. The next evening, she came to my apartment and took me to the church. I met many refugees just like me in the program. It was a beautiful atmosphere of learning, and I told myself that this was my crucial first step.

The classes started at seven o'clock in the evening every day, five days a week. But I had a problem; I had no vehicle, so I couldn't go to school by myself. My brother was busy working. His friend was willing to help me on her day off; the rest of the days I might have to walk to school. It could take over an hour of walking; but I didn't mind. I would do what I had to do to learn how to speak, read, and write the English language well. That was my determination.

Day in and day out, I concentrated on learning English. It was very rough because many nights I didn't have a ride to school and I had to walk. Some days I walked in the rain for over an hour. Even with my umbrella, I got all wet by the time I arrived to my classroom but I was still very happy. If I could learn one new vocabulary and know how to use it, I would be very happy with myself no matter how many miles I walked in the rain. But learning never seemed as easy as I'd thought it would be. I studied a lot. I practiced speaking English with myself very hard; and I thought I should be comfortable with speaking Basic English, but I was wrong.

Sometimes I would go shopping at the supermarket, and when I'd get in line to pay for my merchandise, I'd be excited for the opportunity to have some real-life English practice by exchanging words with the cashier. I wanted to test myself and see how good my English was. Many times I was met with disappointment because I still didn't understand what the cashier was saying. I couldn't catch up; she spoke too quickly. I felt frustrated and embarrassed that I could not comprehend normal conversations.

As I continued to study ESL at the church, I started making friends and learned new things from them. One day I was glad to find out about a program called General Education Development (GED) that would allow me to earn the equivalent of a high school diploma. One of my friends from the ESL class introduced me to another refugee friend who was about to register for the GED classes in a distant campus. I immediately asked for the contact information of that person so I could call and make friends with him.

I called the next day. He and I spoke and we get to know each other; then I asked him the information about the GED classes. He told me he was going to register for classes in a few days in a small and far-away campus sponsored by the Texas Department of Education. When he said the campus was far away, I asked him how far was far away, wondering whether I could walk to campus and how long it would take. He laughed at me and told me no one could walk to the campus from where I lived, as it was about a forty-minute drive and, as the campus was on the other side of the city, it would take more than one freeways to get there. He advised me not to walk to the campus and mentioned that there was no easy bus route either; he had checked and he knew.

The conversation made me feel desperate, but at the end of the talking, he revealed good news. He told me he was willing to help me. He had lived in the States for almost two years. He had a job in a hotel and he had a car. His apartment was not too far from my apartment— only a twenty-minute walk. He suggested that I should walk to his apartment early in the morning and then I could share the ride with him to the GED campus. When the classes were over, he could take me home to my apartment before he headed to work. I was very happy for the offer, and I appreciated him so much for helping me out. He also gave me a fair warning—sometimes he needed to work overtime to earn extra money, and he would have to skip school so he wouldn't be able to take me to school for those days. I told him that was understandable and I had no problem with that. I thanked him, and I couldn't ask for more than he had already offered me.

We both went to the campus two days later to register our classes. It was a small campus, but it looked very well organized and a beautiful learning environment. I met a few teachers, and they welcomed their students with open arms. Their smiles were like blooming flowers in the spring, inviting students to their classes. Their warm greeting made me really excited, and I couldn't wait to sit down and listen to their teachings. I also met a lot of people. The majority were Vietnamese refugees. The rest were other nationalities. The first day of school wasn't far away; the session would start at the beginning of next week.

When the first day of school arrived, I got up very early that Monday morning. I took a long walk to my friend's apartment. I arrived to his place and met several people in his small apartment. They all were up and getting ready for work or school. My friend walked out with two cups of coffee in his hand. He gave me one, and we both got in his car.

The first day of school was great, and the following days and weeks were beautiful. The atmosphere was dynamic and energetic. Everyone paid a great deal of attention in all subjects. Because this was general education, we had to learn many different subjects, along with English. I loved all the subjects, but the most crucial element for me at this time was English. I felt so much more confident to speak, read, and write English now. I took advantage of having mixed nationalities in our classes; it forced me only to speak in English. I knew that the more I spoke, the better I became.

Once I spoke and somebody understood; I wanted to speak more. I was just like a toddler who was learning how to talk. Once a toddler is able to make some noise and somebody listen, he or she would keep talking like a bird keeps singing and won't stop.

Many times I thought about having a girlfriend of a different nationality would give me opportunities to practice speaking English much more. I looked around, but I failed to make any connection. I was either too shy or not brave enough to go forward. Nevertheless, I was very happy to be here. I thanked my friend who gave me rides every day. My goal was to learn and study hard; at the end of this school year, I should be able to pass my GED state exam so I could move on to college.

It was almost six months and the school year came to an end. I needed to get ready for the GED exam. I was very confident that I would pass the exam without any problem. My teachers also told me that I was fully prepared. I wanted to thank all of my GED teachers for all their hard work teaching many of the foreigners to speak proper English so that we could move on to our futures in this great, free nation.

We had a little party on the last day of school. This beautiful place really warmed my heart for my first period of my lifelong journey in this country.

I moved on and took the Texas State Board GED Exam. Indeed, I passed the test. I was extremely happy, and now I could consider myself a high school graduate. It was my very first stepping-stone.

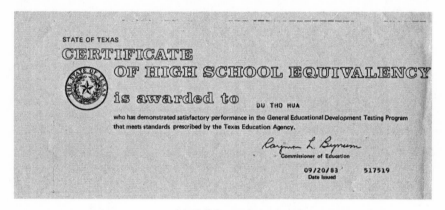

STATE OF TEXAS

CERTIFICATE

OF HIGH SCHOOL EQUIVALENCY

is awarded to   DU THO HUA

who has demonstrated satisfactory performance in the General Educational Development Testing Program that meets standards prescribed by the Texas Education Agency.

Commissioner of Education

09/20/83   517519
Date Issued

My G.E.D certificate.

Now I could go forward and get ready for college; but I already saw many barriers in front of me. First of all, I had been living with my brother for a year, and I totally depended on him. He had just had a baby girl, so now his family grew, and he needed to take care of his family. I didn't feel right continuing to rely on him and going to school. In addition, I didn't have a car. How could I go to college? I didn't even have a driver's license yet. Those were the tough obstacles I had to face.

Then I had a very good idea. Perhaps my brother should send me to a college, where I should stay in a dorm; that could easily to solve my problems. I had heard a lot of good things about the colleges in the northern states. They had good quality education and they were willing to help poor students who wanted to study very hard. I could also find work around the school so I could survive while attending college. I asked my brother to send me to Green Bay, Wisconsin, because he lived there for a while and he still had a few friends living there. Wisconsin was a great state that had many great colleges. My brother didn't answer me, and I thought he needed to think about my request.

A few days later at our dinner table, he told me that he had done a lot of thinking about sending me away to college. He understood my ambition to get a higher education. He would be glad to see me go to college, but sending me so far away would worry him. Then he told me that he had a plan. He wanted me to stay in Houston and attend the local college. He would teach me how to drive and he would also try to find an old car for himself so he could let me borrow his newer car to go to school. I went along with his idea and thanked him for his thoughtfulness.

My brother, his wife, their baby girl, and I at church on a special Sunday.

I finally got my driver's license. He also bought himself a very old car just for the means of his transportation. He handed me the key of his newer car. What he did really affected me. I had created a burden on him, and he didn't mind. I believe he wanted to see his youngest brother succeed in his new life.

XIII

My brother had helped me to get set up for going to college. I just opened the very first chapter of my college life. I was very excited about taking this next step of higher education. I started going to the main campus of the Houston Community College (HCC) and asking a lot of questions about registration, curricula, and financial aid. I also had several friends who had the same goal, and we got together often to support of each others and share new ideas and directions. After a lot of thinking, I chose to pursue the field of mechanical engineering. But before getting into engineering, I needed to take all the basic college classes. I started registering for classes in English, math, and chemistry at HCC.

I was doing very well in most of my classes. Only my English classes gave me trouble. I had no problem making good grades in my other subjects, but I had a tough time making decent grades in my English courses. That bothered me quite a lot, but I refused to give up. I would keep striking harder and harder.

While I was attending the college, I knew that I needed to work to make money to cover my small expenses. At the same time, I needed to share the expenses at home with my brother. Showing my contribution would make me feel a little better while living with his family.

I took a job as an attendant in a huge Laundromat. I was happy that I could work, even though I was only getting paid at a minimum wage. My duties were to maintain the functioning of the washers and dryers, give changes to customers, keep the entire Laundromat and restrooms clean, and fold a lot of clothes. It was very tough because the place was far away from home, and I had to work around my full-time student schedule. Whenever I came to the Laundromat, there was tons of hard work waited there for me. There was time I had to mop the entire floor while keeping my eyes on the customers and machines. Other times, people and children made the mess in the restrooms, I had to get them all cleaned. In addition, I had to clean all the dryer filters once in every few days. They were very dusty, and full of lint. When it was time to do that task, I had to put on a mask. Otherwise, I would breathe in a lot of dust through my mouth and nose.

One positive thing about the cleaning the dryer filters was that I got to collect all the coins and dollar bills that stuck to the filter areas. Sometimes I collected enough money to buy me a lunch for that day.

This reminded me of the days I'd lived in my poor village in the countryside with the Communists. As I found and picked up a coin lying in the bottom of the dryer, the vivid images of those tough times reappeared in my mind; that when I'd tried to help my parents find food for my family by going to the already harvested potato or rice fields and collecting the leftovers. Many times, I hardly collected any rice or potatoes to bring home to my mother. The wounds were still there, and remembering those darkest days hurt deep in my soul.

The semesters came and went. I had settled into routines. I went to school, worked, and studied. I was very happy and doing well in school. I made the dean's list every semester, and I felt very proud. I wished my parents were here so they could see how hard I worked and study. They would be so proud of me. I missed them dearly, and I didn't know if I would ever see them again. I wondered how they were doing. One day that passed was one day my parents got older and their health would deteriorate. I worried most for my father. I had recently received a letter from him and he'd stated that he had some health issues.

I wished I had some money to send them. I was poor to the bone, and I felt bad that I wasn't able to help and support them at this time. I didn't know what to do. If I kept going to school and following the track toward mechanical engineering, I would be going to school for many more years beyond the community college level. I wondered if I should stay on the same track and keep being poor while my family in Vietnam needed my help.

One day I met several of my friends. We sat around a table and discussed a lot of things about school. A few of my friends mentioned an area that really sparked my interest—the computer field. In the '80s, the computer science field was starting to grow and become popular among college students. One good thing was that, if I chose to pursue the field in computers, I could take a two-year program for programmers, majoring in data processing. I could finish the program more quickly and, hopefully, find a better job. I thought that was a good idea. One day, I went to the main college office and changed my plan of study—I would seek a degree in associate's of applied science in data processing—so I could qualify for financial aid.

I started the new semester with a brand-new plan. I had to follow a plan and register for all the required classes. These classes included math, English, accounting, computer, and some others. I was very excited but anxious at the same time. My weakest point was still English. I worried I might not be able to understand all the lectures fully, especially now that I had stepped up to a higher level of difficulty in these technical courses. I knew that I had to study harder. But would that be enough for me to pass these classes? Whatever it took, I told myself that I was ready to take on the challenge and I was confident that I was going to succeed.

The semester started, and I was ready. Things were going very well because I had really prepared. Many times I tried to read the materials beforehand, and that made it easier for me to keep up with all the lectures. Other times, I brought a voice-recording machine so I could record the lecture and listen again later if understanding the teacher in class was difficult for me. I worked very hard at this, but I knew it would pay off. The harder I studied, the more I learned. I made good grades for all my classes. I was extremely happy that I was able to maintain my GPA and remain on the Dean's list.

As I went further along with my curriculum, I had to take computer classes in mainframe and micros. I liked these computer languages. I knew that, if I understood the logic well, I could write any computer programs. I loved these classes so much that I got a part-time job as a computer assistant for the computer labs on campus. Now I was able to help my fellow students. Since I had a small job with the college, it was time for me to quit the cleaning job at the Laundromat. I was so glad I was no longer working as the Laundromat attendant.

Furthermore, some of my fellow students needed more help, and they asked me to tutor them, especially for the microcomputer programs such as dBase and Lotus. They were my favorites computer languages at that time. I was very delighted and pleased that I could help some people. This gave me the very first sense of helping others since I lived in this country.

Things were going extremely well. I was very content with myself. I felt as if I had better control over my own reality. I was still a refugee, but I was able to manage my life fairly well here in my new country. However, sometimes my feelings suddenly turned blue. I still missed my family so much. Getting up every day, I wondered the health of my parents. We all were so far apart, and I didn't know what I should do to show that how much I loved them. I was still very poor and couldn't help them in any way at this time; but I did know that they would be very proud of me, and I intended to continue to demonstrate my hard work while living in my new country.

I also had been missing my girlfriend. It had been several months, and I hadn't received any letter from her, even though I wrote her regularly. I wondered what she was up to. I hoped she was doing all right and continuing to try and escape. Somehow I was still dreaming that she would flee from the Communists and come to America.

My plan of study almost came to an end. I only had one more term left; then I would graduate. It was time for me to look around for a real job. As I was finishing up my last semester, one of my fellow students informed me that there was a nonprofit organization that needed a computer person. I immediately went to the office of the organization—VIP Non-profit Organization—and turned in my résumé.

The director of the organization called me the following week for an interview. I was so excited for my very first job interview. The director offered me the job. I was so happy, even though it was just an entry-level paying job, and I couldn't wait to tell my brother. The first thing that came to my mind was that, if I worked a full-time job, I would be able to save some money and buy me a used car, so I could return my brother his car because I didn't want him to drive a very old car anymore.

I finally finished the curriculum and graduated with an associate's of applied science in data processing with high honors, and I had just stepped onto another stepping-stone. I was very excited about the direction of my life. I started working at VIP Non-profit Organization as a microcomputer programmer. My job was to design the database for the organization and write various simple programs for payroll to our clients.

Things went smoothly and my co-workers were very nice and friendly. I learned a lot about the real nature of business working at the nonprofit company. But then I got an unexpected call to the director's office. I was really anxious to find out what was happening. I had only been working with the organization for several months and things going seemed quite all right. I stepped in the office and the director asked me to have a seat.

She then broke out very bad news for me. She said she had a very small organization and that she'd thought she would expand her business but things were going in the opposite direction. Now she had to lay me off because her business was shrinking. I was very surprised, but nothing I could say. I thanked her for the opportunity and wished her the best for her organization.

I felt very downhearted. I thought I had been on my way to building up my confidence—to be a hard worker and good citizen in my new country. I had been so happy when the American Embassy had accepted me to settle in the United States of America at last, and I had vowed to myself that I would do all I could to show my deepest appreciation and great respect for the country I loved. Although I was just a refugee, I felt I had a responsibility to do my duty fully. The *Cap Anamur* had rescued me in the unforgiving sea so that I could be alive today but the United States had rescued my soul by giving me a life of freedom and dignity. I hoped nothing could take that away for as long as I lived.

Being laid off from my first job had made me think a lot. I felt like something was pushing me down and rejecting me—now I couldn't hold my first job even though I had studied and worked so hard. Something was deterring me from serving the people who had been helping me every step of the way since my new motherland had accepted me. I became very depressed.

Then one night I woke up in the middle of the night. Something clicked in my brain—I could serve the American people by joining the United States Navy. I loved the military. When I was a young boy I saw my brother who was in the South Vietnamese Army and had been wounded in combat, I had promised myself I would join him on the front line when I grew up and that, together, we could protect freedom and maintain democracy for Vietnam. But my fatherland had fallen into the hands of Communists. Now I had my new motherland, and she had accepted me as her new son. The new son ought to serve the new land and help protect freedom and promote democracy throughout the world. Yes! I had made my decision; I would join the United States Navy now when I was young and carry out my own strong beliefs.

When I got up in the morning, I tried to remember everything I had thought about last night. I recalled all of my thinking, and my spiritual mood suddenly changed. I totally forgot my dejection over having been laid off. I wasn't thinking about that anymore, and I was feeling good. I kept the idea and processed it in my mind for a few days before I told my brother, even though I believed I really liked my decision and I was going to make it happen in the new days to come.

A few days later at the dinner table with my brother's family, I shared my idea. I told him I wanted to join the US Navy. My brother was totally surprised. I caught him off guard. He knew that I was trying to find another job, but the economy at this time was very sluggish and I couldn't find one. He told me that joining the US Navy was a huge decision for me. He said entering the military would be very rough. He knew this from his own experience, although he had joined the South Vietnamese Army in his native country.

He claimed that entering military service would be so much harder for me when I had only lived in this country for a few years and, in his eyes, I was still a refugee. I was still learning English. How would I deal with the language barrier in the tough training environment of the United States Navy? In addition, he also mentioned that matching my physical abilities with my fellow American service members would be a very harsh experience. I was a skinny guy, and I only weighed 120 pounds at the time. He added that the American traditions and customs would be all new to me. How I would be able to get through the US Navy training physically and emotionally? My brother raised a lot of concerns, and he wasn't sure that joining the US Navy was a solid, good decision for me.

I listened to my brother; what he said was right, and I respected all his opinions and ideas. I told him that I wanted to serve my new country. I understood all his concerns, but he also needed to listen to me and hear what I had to say. I told him that it had taken eleven attempts before I had been able to escape the Communist regime and I had finally succeeded. I also told my brother that, as just a young teenager, I had been able to learn to become a marine engine mechanic. That was also a tough task, but I had become a good one.. I had installed several engines from scratch on my own, and my skill had helped me to reach to the land of freedom.

All I wanted to tell my brother that I had a strong will. I assured him that I knew I would have to encounter a lot of barriers, suffering, and difficulties, but I would receive great learning and training in return. All I needed to do was to put my mind to it and concentrate on my goal. If I could do that, I knew I would achieve my purpose. I was now only in my mid-twenties, and I was sure I could do this. Finally, I thanked my brother for all his concerns, but I had made up my mind. I just wanted him to be happy and allow his youngest bother to join the United States Navy.

While I was thinking about the enlistment with U.S. Navy, I received wonderful news from West Germany. My brother-in-law had sponsored the remainder of his family in Vietnam, and they had all gone to West Germany. His wife, his youngest son, and three daughters had finally reunited with him. My sister and her children flew from Vietnam to West Germany. They didn't have to escape the country, risking their lives and suffering like my brother-in-law and I had. This was the happiest day for my sister's family. The tough times that had resulted from her family being apart were coming to an end. I was very happy for them and I offered congratulations. My sister's entire family was finally out of the hands of the Vietnamese Communists. Nothing else could be better than the entire family reaching freedom like they ever had dreamed. I was so excited for them.

I wanted to see my sister and her family before joining the US Navy. I had been missing them very much. I felt I needed to be with them to share our feelings about the darkest days of our lives and to reconnect the bonds that we had all missed for all those years. I decided to arrange a trip to West Germany.

I saved some money for the ticket to see my sister. One beautiful day, I took off for West Germany. It was not that long a flight. Before long, the airplane had landed in a beautiful airport in Stuttgart, West Germany. I walked out of the gate, and there they were—the whole family was standing and waiting to see me. What a special moment that was. No words could describe our emotions at that time. I just couldn't believe I was seeing my sister's entire family in one piece again. This was a miracle. I gave each and every one of them a long hug. This was a great day.

I stayed a few weeks with my sister's family. We talked a lot. I asked my sister about her struggles after her husband had escaped from Vietnam. She said it had been very difficult. Suddenly, her husband and oldest son had just disappeared from the family. But just thinking about the future of her children, she was able to hang on so she could see the much better fate of her destiny. Indeed, she was a strong woman and was able to overcome all major obstacles in her life. And the rewards were clear—the family was here together and their future held a lot of promise. All of the sacrifices and suffering had paid off. They had their lives in a great new country, their freedom and the great prospect for their family. This was priceless.

My sister also asked me if I still kept in touch with my girlfriend. I told her I hadn't received any letters from her for a long time, although I kept writing to her. I had lost touch with her, and I wondered how she was doing now. My sister told me that, in the days after my escape, my girlfriend became very friendly with my sister's family. During that time, my mother had come to live with my sister. One day, my mother had gotten very ill. She had a lot of swelling and pain in her right breast area. My girlfriend was working in a hospital nearby and she knew some good doctors. She took my mother to see a doctor for an examination. The doctor said my mother had breast cancer.

My mother was very lucky because the doctor had caught the cancer just before it became spreading. My girlfriend, just like a daughter, had taken care of my mother and saved her life. I was shocked and affected by the story my sister was telling me. I told my sister that I owed my girlfriend my deepest gratitude. I hoped that one day I could see her and thank her for saving my mother.

I only had a few more weeks in Germany before I would head back to the United States. I wanted to visit some of the people in my boat group before going back to the States. Most of them lived in the central and northern parts of West Germany. I made the trip to see them. It was great see each other again for the first time since we were together in the refugee camp.

I also got to do some sightseeing. Many of the historical places were incredible. I had a chance to go to West Berlin. Several of my friends and I got together to make a special trip and traveled to the capital West Berlin by car. We drove normally on the beautiful freeways of West Germany. Then we had to stop at the gate, where I saw the East Berlin Communist soldiers, and they asked us for our traveling documents. A strange feeling hit the pit of my stomach as this made me recall the Communists in Vietnam. After passing the checkpoint of the East German Communists, I asked my friends whether we knew what we were doing. We had gone through life-and-death experiences to escape the Communists; we certainly didn't want to have anything to do with the Communists of East Berlin. Everybody in the car laughed out loud because they knew I was making a sarcastic joke.

Driving on the road of the East Berlin side, I had a very strange feeling because the atmosphere had totally changed. The signs and activities on the streets were so odd and different; the green color of life barely touched the landscape. I saw only black and white street signs with fences, barriers, and barbed wires. I could feel the tension in the air as we were traveling on the East German streets.

We drove for a few hours before we came to the other gate of East Germany. Here again, we had to show documents. Once we were in the city of West Berlin, the atmosphere changed back to live and vibrant nature of the free enterprise of this beautiful city.

Over the next few days, I got to see a lot of things around this gorgeous city. Many of the beautiful buildings and churches were historically popular. Most important of all, all of my friends and I went to see the Berlin Wall. The wall was very tall with barbed wire at the top, and it was very long across the border. This wall had divided the country of Germany into East and West. The East German Communists had put up this shameful wall in 1961 to prevent the East Germans from escaping the Communists and seeking freedom in West Berlin.

Memorial of the Victims of the Wall.

I also happened to see several of the graves of the East German people who were buried next to the wall on the west side. These people had shown their bravery by climbing up the wall in an attempt to escape the Communists, but the East German Communist soldiers had shot and killed them. They felt down on the west side of the wall. I could relate the fates between these escapees and the Vietnamese boat people. They unfortunately got shot and killed while we were lucky to escape the Vietnamese Communist regime. They were about my age, and they had attempted to cross the wall about five years ago. They had chosen to die rather than to live with the barbaric Communists. I kneeled down and pressed my hand against these gravesite memorials, paying my respect.

Standing on the west side of the Berlin Wall.

Witnessing the graves of these East Germans made me reflect. History had truly shown that Communism was bad news for mankind. So why did Communism still exist? In Vietnam, when the country had been divided into north and south, huge waves of North Vietnamese people had flooded into the south so they could live freely. The division of the country had come by an agreement and the people who chose freedom could move to the south and live happily. But the Communists of Vietnam had disregarded the agreement and had shown their aggression to the highest level so that they could take over the south.

As a result, many of the elder Vietnamese citizens had had to escape the Communist regime twice. They had first escaped from the north into the south in 1954 when the country was divided; and they had had to escape a second time after the Fall of Saigon in 1975.

It was so obvious that the Communists had destroyed the democracy of my people and taken away their freedom, showing no regard for dignity of mankind. It was clear that Communism was bad news for our universe; therefore, Communism should not exist on our planet.

I had a good time in Berlin with a lot of my friends. I learned a lot about this magnificent city. I was glad I made the trip. It was time for me to go back to my sister's home near Stuttgart. Then I had to finish up my trip in Germany and prepare to go back home to the United States of America.

XIV

$\mathscr{B}$ack home in Houston, Texas, one day, I watched on television as our president, Ronald Reagan, made big news in West Berlin. Our president ordered Mr. Gorbachev, the Russian Communist leader, to tear down the shameful Berlin Wall. I couldn't believe this. I was just there not too long ago. President Ronald Reagan was my hero. What he said there was the beginning of the symbolic reunification of West and East Germany, and eventually the Berlin Wall would come down and our president would liberate millions of East Germans from the evil East Germany Communist Party.

"Mr. Gorbachev, tear down this wall."

The time had come; I needed to complete the paperwork so I could start my new adventure and join the US Navy. I went to the Navy recruiting office in downtown Houston, signed my enlistment, and swore in and I completed the process. One of the chief of recruiting officers asked me what I wanted to do in the Navy. I told him that I had a two-year computer degree, so I wanted to specialize in computer sciences for the Navy. He checked and told me I had a problem. Specializing in computers would require me to be a US citizen, since the computer specialists received a high security clearance. At this point, I was still a refugee with a green card. I was disappointed, but it didn't really matter in my thinking. All I wanted to do was serve in the U.S. Navy.

The chief asked me what would be my second choice. I told him I used to be a mechanic in Vietnam, and I asked him for suggestion. He mentioned that I could become a mechanic and fix fighting jet or helicopter engines. I thought that would be very exciting. I had always wanted to work with airplanes.

Finally, I chose my career with the US Navy as an aviation machinist mate or AD

The chief gave me the date to enter the Navy boot camp. That day—a day in May 1987—was not far away. Next week, I would fly to the Naval Training Center in Orlando, Florida, for my basic training.

The day of enlistment in the US Navy.

That day, I got up very early to make coffee and waited for my brother to get up to take me to the airport. When my brother walked out of his room, I handed him a cup of coffee; then we were on our way to Houston International Airport. He walked with me to the gate. He gave me a big hug and asked me to be really careful. He wished me luck, and I thanked him for all the times he had been supporting me. I knew that I would be on my own from now on. We said good-bye, and he stood there, watching his brother disappear through the boarding gate.

During the flight, so many thoughts ran through my head. I wanted to devote myself to what I believed. But who knew what my future would hold? I did what I thought and believed to be right, but whether I would get the results I expected was a totally different thing. I knew I was just a refugee, but I had big dreams. I strongly believed that every one of us who was living on this earth and breathing the same air on this planet should have the responsibility and the respect to each other so we could build harmony for the lives among us. Then we would achieve true happiness in return.

But it was not that simple, and life was much more complicated than anyone thought. Most of us knew that Communism was bad news for humankind. Its theories and philosophies were just like creating heaven for all humanity, but its application was totally opposite. Individuals who devoted and dedicated their lives to Communism had evil minds that would easily trap innocent people in their dark world.

I had suffered so much because of the Communist regime and, as a result, I felt strongly that I should have the responsibility to help protect the foundation of freedom. I hoped I would never have to see or live with Communists ever again.

Today turned a brand new chapter in my life. I knew this was going to be tough and difficult direction but it would include responsibilities and dignity. I praised God, asking him to help me to overcome the challenging road ahead.

Soon the airplane landed in the Orlando International Airport. I was anxious to see what would happen next. I found my group who were in the same position as I was, and we all headed to the bus outside of the airport. It took us to the Naval Training Center.

As soon as the door of the bus opened, I heard the yelling, screaming and giving orders from the company commanders who were already there and waiting for us. We all quickly lined up and followed the commands. I was shocked. I had just entered a totally different world. I tried to keep my head up and listen to those orders and carried out the commands. For some of the orders, I had no idea what the commander was talking about. I got really scared and nervous.

I immediately had second thoughts. Would this be the right place for me? Had I made the right decision coming here? But now was no time to think; I had to pay 110 percent attention to what was going on around me; otherwise, I would be screamed at very bad

The first three days were worse than hell. We had no sleep or rest. We did a million things in one day. We got our heads shaved completely. I was shocked to see my baldhead in the mirror. We stood in line to get personal supplies and uniforms. It was one thing after another, and we had to do everything quick, quick, quick. At times, the commanders made us stand at attention for hours under the hot sun of the Sunshine State and listen to the company commanders lecturing. If any of us made any movement, we would be asked to drop and do many push-ups. They could scream at us for anything.

These company commanders were here for a sole purpose—to transform all the men and women into sailors. But before they could do that, they had to break down all of our personalities and smash our egos into pieces. They had to destroy all of our pride and self-respect. They made us feel like we were nothing—that we would exist only if we followed their orders. They made us think and feel that we were smaller than a grain of sand in the desert. We'd better just listened up.

These company commanders were Gods and Goddesses. We had to totally devote ourselves to them under whatever conditions. We had to carry out their orders with the greatest effort.

But one time, after all of the yelling and screaming, one of my company commanders had us all standing at attention. He asked us if we knew what we were here for. Then he answered his own question, talking loudly. "*The reason you are here because your country needs you,*" he boomed. He went on about how it was our responsibilities to protect our greatest nation.

Then, in a sudden movement, the company commander stepped to the corner of the room; everyone became completely silent, and the sound of music started to drift into the room. The music grew louder and louder, echoing and filling the barrack with the song "God Bless America."

Oh my God! I could not hold my emotion it. Tears dripped from my eyes. I had heard this song since I lived in this country, and it was one of my favorite America's songs. This was the best timing; I needed to hear the song again. As the song was playing, my feelings were pouring into my new motherland; she meant so much to me. Without this nation, I wouldn't be here standing in freedom, and the Communists would spread all over the world. *God bless America, land that I loved, from the mountains to the prairies.* I would do anything to help protect her, the United States of America. *God gave me liberty or God gave me death.* I knew the coming days were going to be very tough, but it was okay for me. I had to realize that this was a Navy boot camp.

Throughout the days of training, I also thought much about my first country, Vietnam. I missed my parents, and they probably got very old. They wouldn't know I had joined the US Navy to fight for their own beliefs. They would have been very proud of their son who had figured out a way to escape the Communists and found freedom in America; then their youngest son was willing to dedicate himself to join the U.S. Navy in order to help protect that freedom. I believed they would be very delightful to see what I was doing now.

A few weeks of training had passed and one day my company commander informed me that I had a visitor waiting to see me at the training center. I was so surprised that someone was visiting me, and I wondered who it could be. My only family member in this country was my brother living in Houston, and he had to work every day to support his family. It couldn't possibly be him; nevertheless, I hoped that it was he because I missed him very much especially at this time. I remembered when he had joined the South Vietnamese Army; my mother had been there for him, supporting him along every step of his training. It was a totally different story for me now. My parents were living in the other side of the planet, and I expected to be on my own here in my new country. If I could see my brother today that would be a priceless gift he would give to me. While walking to the center, I was excited and anxious to find out whom it was to see me.

When I got there, I found out it was my brother's friend. His name is Loc who came to Orlando to visit his own family. Because I knew him through my brother, he had just swung by to visit me in the boot camp. I was disappointed that wasn't my brother but the visiting of my brother's friend was still very emotional for me. My tears almost fell but I held them in. I gave him a big hug and thanked him for thinking of me while visiting his family in Orlando. Before we said good-bye, I asked him to give my brother and his family my best regards and tell them that I missed them. I also told him that the camp was very tough, and I would do my best to get through the training.

Things started getting a little better but were still very rough and very intense. I tried very hard to fit into the groove. Many early mornings, our company commanders would come to the barracks around four o'clock and wake us up by slamming the big, aluminum trash cans on the floor. The noise was excruciating and horrible. We were all freak out, thinking that somebody was breaking the building into pieces.

I took it one day at a time. We trained heavily every day. I worried I wouldn't hold up physically. We only slept a few hours each night, and every day was the dedication of intensive physical training. I became very sick and developed pneumonia. I even coughed up my own blood. My body couldn't tolerate the extreme cold of the very early mornings and the extreme heat of the afternoons. Another factor that contributed to my illness was that I had a bad habit of smoking. When I was young, everybody said that every man needed to smoke. Even though I didn't smoke much because there was hardly any smoking breaks allowed, I still believe the smoking contributed to my ill condition at this time.

My company commanders allowed me to go to the sick hall and have a few days of rest. Those few days of treatment took care of my problems, and I got my strength back.

To make it even better, I decided to quit smoking cold turkey. Many of my smoking fellows didn't think that I would be able to quit. I told them that, if I said I would quit smoking, I would do it. Indeed, my determination prevailed. I quit smoking from that day on. I had absolutely no temptation to return to smoking. I was so glad I did it. I had done myself for my health and my wellness when I needed the most. I felt so much better and so much stronger. I felt that I was ready to take orders from my company commanders once again.

Days came and went. Each day that passed was a big reward for me. We all counted the days to the day of graduation. Honestly, I loved all the training. I loved when we marched together on the street. I had a lot of fun. I loved the military exercises such as shooting, swimming, fire fighting and so on. I loved it when we worked together as a team; every step or task of every individual was moving at the same beat. We worked together and we were at the same wavelengths so that we get things done in a desirable and remarkable way. This was why the United States of America was so great; everybody loved the freedom of enterprise of this country. Together as a team we could make this one nation the greatest.

Time to march to chow hall.

One day came and it brought bad news. That day, we all had to take the basic academic tests and pass before we could move on with our training. I took the tests. I passed all the subjects except I stumbled and failed the part of English reading. This really bothered me, but nothing much I could do.

I tried my best. Anyone who had just learned a new language, especially as an adult, had to pass a standard reading test would be a very tough task.

Now I had to encounter the setback; I was removed from my present company and sent to a remedial reading session for a few weeks. This was a little bit upsetting, but I decided to look at it in a different way, a good way. I had a chance to improve my English while I stayed in the Navy boot camp. In addition, in my fate, I knew that the road I was on would have a lot of challenges and obstacles. I had to accept my own status and keep my mind open so I could face the reality and move on.

Physical training time.

A few weeks passed, and I completed the remedial session. Now I was assigned to a new company (C014) so I could go on with my trainings. The extreme heat of Orlando had taken a toll on the new sailors, but nothing could stop me from moving forward. The shock of the rigor of Navy training had caused me to hesitate at first, but then I had determined to learn quickly. The Navy had taught me so much about core values, working as a team, and leadership. Every day I kept learning new things about myself through physical training and Navy disciplines.

One of my favorite training sessions was shooting. I followed the instructions from the trainer. I made sure I knew how to hold the pistol and aim at the target correctly. I started firing, and all my shots hit the prime target. The trainer was really impressed, and he accused me of being a real killer. I thanked him for the compliment. I related this to real life. If I had the disciplines, knew how to follow directions, and concentrate, I could achieve my goals no matter how difficult the task was.

My boot camp company, C014

Ready for graduation.

My trainings had almost come to an end, and graduation was near. I was very excited for what was coming, especially graduation. Somehow, I had a special and wonderful feeling; not only were the doors just about to open for my future, but so too were my soul and my spirit. In just another week, I would become a sailor in the United States Navy. I would be so proud to be committed to the most powerful military on this earth—to defend and protect my new, beloved nation. It was just like a dream.

Several years ago, it seemed like yesterday that I was a little boy living under the brutal policies of the Vietcong; but today, in my soul and spirit, I had spread and soared my wings into the blue sky of freedom above the magnificent mountains and shining seas of this great nation. It was almost midnight and I was lying on my rack and trying to get some sleep, my hand on my forehead, telling myself that tomorrow would be even a brighter day.

Graduation time.

Indeed, graduation was here. I could see that everyone's face was smiling and everybody's spirit was uplifted, including mine. The anticipation was building very high. The transformation from civilian to sailor was almost complete. The final mile of the beginning stage of naval career journey loomed very near. I couldn't wait to put on my formal, white sailor uniform and march in front of admirals, captains, and spectators. Every single one of us looked great in our uniforms. It was time for everyone to be in array and ready for the most important march of our lives.

I was so excited, but I was also 100 percent attentive. We followed the recruit company commander and marched to the huge stadium for the graduation ceremony. Wow! What a spectacular view it was. The endless hours of tough training, routine, and practice were now blooming in the display of the prestigious uniforms of the shining and gorgeous faces of these young sailors. The ceremony began with the national anthem. The beautiful voices of the recruit bluejacket chorus echoed through the entire stadium while my hand saluted the American flag. My emotions were high during this special moment. I had accepted this nation as my own, so I vowed to fight for my new beloved country. I would take the honor and bear true faith and allegiance. I would have the courage to support and defend. I would honor my commitment to obey and follow orders.

The special teams passed in front of us one by one. The beautiful flag team carried the fifty flags of our fifty states, showing so much pride. The Naval

Training Music Band walked by with the strong beats and magnificent sound of the music. Next came the drill team. Their performance with quickness and precision was so impressive.

Finally came the Pass-In-Review. Company after company marched passing the reviewing stand. Then it was our company's turn to march. I was prideful beyond my ability to describe. If my parents were here, they would be so proud of me.

Pass-In-Review.

When the ceremony was over, we marched back to our barracks. It was time to celebrate the job well done and the mission accomplished. The atmosphere was incredibly happy and beautiful. Young, brand-new sailors in white uniforms, along with their family and friends filled the naval center. It was a great day. I knew that the parents were very proud of their sons and daughters on this day of achievement. I was so happy for all my shipmates.

I looked around me, but none of my family members were with me. If my mother were here, she would embrace me tightly in her arms and she would have a beautiful smile of pride for her youngest son. I really needed her for a moment like this. I missed her. I couldn't hold back the tears when I thought of my mother. I tried to push all the sad feelings away. I told myself I should always think positively in any circumstances. I knew that my family was very happy and proud of me. I had just made my dream come true.

There were a few of my shipmates were just like me, with no family members around. We started talking and making jokes with each other. One shipmate invited me for a cigarette; I had quit smoking, but I took the cigarette from his hand just for this time and we joined in the celebration. I started feeling great again. I felt ecstatic and wonderful to be a member of the United State Navy. I realized I had a long journey lay ahead of me—a journey on which I would serve and protect the most precious principles of humanity, freedom and democracy.

Du Tho Hua, US Navy

XV

My next adventure, seaman school, was just around the corner. First, we were allowed two weeks of vacation. I couldn't wait for this.

I went to Houston to see my brother and his family. His children were getting bigger and bigger. It had only been four months since I left, but it seemed like I hadn't seen them for years. It was so good to be around my brother and his family once again, and it was a perfect time as we were about to share the holiday season together. I got to enjoy his wife's cooking, which I had missed for so long. I planned to chill out and do nothing other than enjoy the holiday spirit and my brother's family until it was time to head back to the Navy world.

The welcome home cake warmed my heart.

Two weeks of vacation went by quickly. I thanked my brother's family for the good times we had shared during the holiday season of 1987. I really appreciated the hospitality I received from my brother, my sister-in-law, and my brother's friends. I considered myself very lucky to have at least one family member living in this country. My brother was the only person I could turn to when I faced difficulties and problems. I thought back that

I had made the right decision to fight with the American Embassy in the refugee camp for my acceptance into this country.

Now that I was no longer living with my brother, from here on out, I would always be a lonely sailor. I had chosen this life because I wanted to follow my own beliefs. After my years of living with the Communist regime, I wanted to show people around me that I had come to freedom from the hell of the Communist regime and that, once I had found freedom, I wanted to protect it just like our forefathers had done—"live free or die."

My seaman classmates and me.

It was time for me to go back to Navy life. I flew back to Orlando for seaman school. This training was short and easy compared to boot camp. I met several of my shipmates from basic training. Now we were together in seaman school. We also had several female shipmates in our class.

In the seaman school, we learned to perform various duties, such as helmsmen and lookout, and how to repair and maintain equipment. We learned how to perform all the preparations to get ships ready and underway. We also seriously learned how to stand watch while in port and underway and so on.

The training was so short that it came to an end without our realizing it. I was voted class leader since I was the oldest. I had a lot of fun and enjoyed the company of my classmates. We were soon to be on our way, going to different Class "A" schools and we would be heading in different directions.

I wished my shipmates luck, and I hoped we would remember each other down the road of our Navy careers.

It was also time for me to say good-bye to Orlando. I would be heading to my class "A" school in Millington, Tennessee—my last training before I would be assigned to a ship or squadron. I arrived in Tennessee in the early spring of 1988, and the weather here was very chilly. I didn't like that because I wasn't used to cold weather.

The training center was very large. Most sailors who chose aviation technical schools had to come here. My field was aviation machinist mate (AD); I was here to learn all about the aircraft engines. I reflected on my previous days as a marine engine mechanic that helped myself to escape the Vietcong Communists. Now I had become a free man living in a free country; I was about to become a jet mechanic that helped to deter any aggression against my new country and protect the core principles of humanity in this world. That had become the most important motivation for me, and I hoped I would become a great aviation machinist mate, just as, once upon a time, I had been a great marine engine mechanic.

My seaman class.

I settled into the checking-in process. I would start my first day of classes in a few days. Aviation machinist mate, school was a very serious Class "A" school. Keeping those aircrafts operating effectively in the air was the utmost important business of the US Navy and what made America the most powerful military on earth. The course would last three months with eight hours daily in class. I knew that it was going to be tough and require a lot of disciplines. The intensity almost matched that of boot camp. Instead of focusing on physical training, we focused on technical aspects and principles.

My aviation machinist mate class.

Once again, I was chosen as the class leader, and I didn't expect that. I had about twenty classmates, including several US Marines. It would be very hard for me to take charge and keep the class in order, especially with the Marines in my class. They always thought they were tougher than anybody else. So how could Navy guy like me with a language barrier to take charge?

I couldn't turn the position down because I had the most education among my classmates. I had no choice but to go forward, overcome all barriers, and show my classmates my leadership. I became stronger and tougher about keeping the class in order as we marched to and from the school center; cleaned the classroom, tools, and equipment; and so on. After all, I was doing well. All of my classmates and I soon became good friends, and we helped each other out when anyone needed help. We also competed with each other academically or during hands-on training. I had a great time, and I enjoyed my class of aviation machinist mates very much.

Class march—one, two, three …

Time flew by when we were having fun. Soon, the class of aviation machinist mate had come to an end. We all had finished and passed all the exams. It was time for us to move on and go our own ways, and everyone was very excited to work on the real aircrafts very soon. I was no exception. We each received our different orders that would take us in different directions. Some of us were sent overseas, while others received orders to station in different squadrons to specialize on different kinds of aircraft.

I received my order to Cecil Field, Florida, with Strike Fighter Squadron VFA-86 that belonged to one of the F/A-18 Hornet fighter jets. I couldn't

The fun times together.

wait to get my hands on the most sophisticated F/A-18 fighter airplanes in the United States Navy. I couldn't wait for my new adventures to begin.

During this final training period, I had met several young Vietnamese sailors who also joined the Navy and had technical school here in Millington, Tennessee. We talked and became friends. I had a lot of admiration for them for working and study very hard to become the best sailors they could be. I felt blessed to meet with them, and it was more fun to have them around. We could relate to each other easily because we shared almost the same background and customs. They were much younger than I was. They had escaped the Communists to come to the United States of America with their families when they were very little boys, and most of their fathers were former South Vietnamese soldiers. They joined the US Navy after they finished their high schools in this country, so most of them didn't have any English language barrier at all.

The night before my last day, we had a little party with instant noodle soups and water. I still remember that night clearly.

I got another chance to take a vacation. I flew to Houston to visit my brother's family again before heading to Cecil Field, Florida. I planned to relax and spend time with my nephew and nieces.

A sailor, also Vietnamese, discussed
my order to VFA-86.

XVI

$\mathscr{T}$wo weeks were gone quickly, and I was eager to explore the new adventures and opportunities ahead of me, especially getting my hands on repair, replace and maintain the fighter jet engines of the Hornet. Before checking into my permanent squadron, I had to attend the introduction course about the F/A-18 with my brother squadron, VFA-106, which was stationed in the same location.

VFA-86 logo.

After a few weeks of indoctrination at the brother squadron, VFA-106, I was ready to check into my home squadron. I arrived at VFA-86 on a beautiful, sunny day. I checked in with the master chief of the squadron, and he took me around, introducing the brand-new, young sailor to the commanders of the squadron and giving me a tour to the entire squadron. I was impressed with the layout and its organization.

The master chief then took me to the hangar; he wanted me to see the F/A-18 Hornets. Wow! They were magnificent. I called them the Iron Hornets. I looked outside of the hangar and saw the line of Hornets standing next to the runway of this huge naval air base. I was stunned.

The Iron Hornets of VFA-86

Suddenly, a flashback from my soul—one of the worst nightmares that I recalled--replayed, I saw the Vietcong's tanks and Communist soldiers marching into Quang Ngai to take over my city. I imagined that, if I could have flown these Hornets, I could have scared the hell of those Communist invaders and pushed them back to where they belonged.

Next, my master chief took me to the aviation machinist mate shop where I belonged. I met my petty officer first-class supervisor and teammates. There were about fifteen of us in the shop. I shook everyone's hands, and the group welcomed me to the unit. I felt very lucky to be here, and I knew that I would have a lot to learn from my teammates.

The transition went smothly as I hoped it was. I soon fell into the normal routines of a regular sailor. I got up early every morning and walked to my squadron from the barracks. Many beautiful mornings bright with Florida sunshine reminded me of Vietnam. As I walked down the road to my shop, I often remembered those days of mechanic's training with my master in my first country. All of those boat mechanic skills were helping me now in some ways, especially when it came to handling tools and hardware. My ocupational background made me felt a little bit more comfortable, even though I knew I have an ocean of learning here.

Now I lived in better, more relaxed environment and atmosphere compared to my technical schools or training camps although it was still in military style. I worked very hard and learned a lot from my shipmates. Maintaining

Strike like sidewinders.

and repairing these magnificent aircrafts, required crucial skills and knowledge. I would try to learn very hard as much as I could so I could become a great technician just like one of my shipmates.

I had been with my squadron for a little while. I had spent many enjoyable hours observing our pilots fly the Hornets. Whenever I had a chance, I liked to watch the pilots flying the planes. Watching them from taking off to landing on the runways was awesome everytime. I really admired those pilots. I couldn't imagine what else they could do. They made me start dreaming of becoming a pilot.

The dream was far beyond my reach, I affraid, but watching these pilots, I aspired to become one—flying like an eagle in the sky with no limit, that would be so sensational. I had some prior college, and if I had a chance to continue my education, I might one day have an opportunity to apply to an officer candidate program.

Very soon, our squadron would have to prepare for important assignments. For one, we were going to participate in military exercises conducted with our alliance of countries from North America and Europe—those who had committed to fulfilling the goals of the North Atlantic Treaty Organization (NATO). The first assignment exercise for the squadron was in Key West Naval Air Station for one week.

My shipmates and I would have to arrive in Key West during the second week of May 1988. I got to fly with my master chief, along with three other sailors in a very small, seven-seater airplane. I was very excited at first, but I became a little bit nervous when I saw such a tiny airplane. But then it didn't bother me after all. I figured this was the US Navy and a naval officer was the pilot of this airplane. I remembered I was brave enough to escape the Communists on a very tiny boat so flying in this small airplane would be just an adventure.

It was beautiful, and sunny day, and I had nothing to worry about but to enjoy this special day of adventure. We all got in the airplane and we took off from Naval Air Station Cecil Field to fly to Naval Air Station of Key West.

The airplane was airborne and continued cutting the air, flying up and up. What a special feeling of excitement! The airplane was just like a little leaf floating in the beautiful, clear sky with seven people on board. I kept smiling because I couldn't believe I was experiencing this kind of adventure in my life. It was hard to describe the sensation of being in the air in a tiny aircraft. I felt like I was Aladdin flying his magic carpet. I reminded myself, *Let's enjoy the magical world.*

Before landing, the pilot circled the gorgeous city so we could see the magnificent view of Key West. From the sky looking down, we saw the beautiful, blue ocean hugging the small, tropical, exotic island—this lagoon was an indescribable view of nature's beauty. Soon, the aircraft had landed safely, and I was so glad I'd made the flight.

We were here for several days, and we had time to enjoy the beautiful weather of Key West. After a hard working day, I tried take the opportunity to explore the exotic city. The water was warm and crystal clear that I could see through the sea bottom. On many evenings, I went to the beautiful beaches and unable to resist the magnificent view of sunsets, I took many beautiful pictures.

Photography was one of my favorite hobbies and I thought that God had made this planet beautiful, and it was up to me to capture the beauty of the universe.

A beautiful sunset of Key West.

The last day of the exercise came quickly. Our squadron had a little picnic to celebrate our hard work and a job well done. We came to a park with a big hut in the middle. The hut, made of straw grass and wooden posts, reminded me of my village in Vietnam. My heart grew heavy as I missed my village and wondered about my parents, as well as my friends and the other villagers. Were they still there? How much were they now suffering? I hoped that, one day, I could go back to see them just one more time.

Hoping I could see my parents one day.

Back to the home base after a week at NAS Key West, we returned to our normal routines. But before long, we would have another exercise to do. Next assignment, our pilots were to conduct exercises at the air force base in Indian Springs, Nevada.

We arrived in Indian Springs, Nevada, during the first week of November 1988. This base was huge and it's geography that was totally new to me. Desert and sparse mountains surrounded the base. There was not much vegetation here; however, I got to see the air force base and I had a chance to explore different types of warplanes. I loved the giant F-15 fighter jets. When an F-15 took off, the earth seemed to shake with its full afterburner throttle. Just looking at the F-15s, it would be very intimidating.

This Air Force base was also the home of impressive F-16s. These Thunderbirds were smaller, single-engine fighter jets with elegant appearance, similar to our Hornets. The planes were all magnificent and splendid. Staying here at the air force base gave me an opportunity to see the extended scope of how powerful this country was. I was very thankful to live in this country and I was very happy and proud to be a member of this nation's armed forces.

Back at Naval Air Station Cecil Field, our shop resumed the normal business of repairing and maintaining our Hornets in our home hangar. There were so much to learn, and I tried to follow one step at a time, learning from my teammates. We were soon to be ready for the North Atlantic Treaty Organization (NATO) cruise, just a few months away.

At this time, I was eligible for advancement in rank. I didn't know I would have the opportunity so soon, but I was very excited for the chance to go up in rank. I had just been an aviation machinist mate airman or ADAN all this time. I would like to become a petty officer and take on more responsibilities and lead others.

I went to the administration office and acquired all the materials I would need to study. I learned that the test for advancement would be in a few weeks, so I really needed to study and focus. I knew it wouldn't easy for me because of my barrier with the English language, but I was going to give it my best shot, and I was confident I would pass the petty officer third class exam.

I got up very early the morning of the test and arrived at the testing center. Hundreds of sailors were there for the advancement exams. I realized this was going to be a real competition. The exam was very long, but because I had studied hard, I was familiar with most of the material. I thought I'd done well, and I hoped for the best.

The holiday season was approaching, and the winter had arrived. But the Sunshine State showed no seasonal indication. The New Year of 1989 was fast approaching, and this year would be the year of action for our squadron. We were going to make a two-month NATO cruise in February, and we would also be making a six-month Mediterranean cruise in May. I was very excited for the squadron's plan. I couldn't wait to arrive on the aircraft carrier. This was going to be my very first cruise, and I was filled with anticipation.

I remembered when I was in Vietnam prior to my escape. I heard so much about the American fleets in the high seas. We knew many of the boat people were fortunate enough to get rescued by the US Navy ships. For that reason, during my escape, the people on my boat prayed to get rescued by American fleets. Even though the American ship didn't rescue my boat but the American fleets had projected the image of angels watching over the helpless boat people on the unforgiving sea. Very soon, I would see and live on a real American fleet. I couldn't imagine what would be more exciting.

XVII

As my shipmates and I prepared for the NATO cruise, I got a call from the petty officer first class in administration. I went to his office and he gave me really good news. I had passed the exam and I was advanced to petty officer third Class (AD3). I was ecstatic. He also told me the ceremony for the advancement would be soon. He congratulated me, and I thanked him for this terrific news.

DEPARTMENT OF THE NAVY
STRIKE FIGHTER SQUADRON EIGHTY-SIX
FPO MIAMI 34099-6220

IN REPLY REFER TO:
1430
10
16 Jan 89

From: Commanding Officer, Strike Fighter Squadron 86
To: ADAN Du T. Hua, USN,

Subj: AUTHORITY TO ASSUME THE TITLE AND WEAR THE UNIFORM OF A
       THIRD CLASS PETTY OFFICER, UNITED STATES NAVY

Ref: (a) MILPERSMAN 2230130

1. Under reference (a), you are hereby authorized to assume the title and wear the uniform of a Petty Officer Third Class effective immediately.

2. Your appointment as a Petty Officer in the United States Navy makes you heir to a long and proud tradition of Naval leadership. By accepting this appointment, you are charged with demonstrating those standards of performance, moral courage, and dedication to the Navy and the Nation which may serve as an enviable example to your fellow Navy men and women.

3. Under reference (a), you will not be entitled to pay and other monetary allowances of a Third Class Petty Officer until actually advanced to the pay grade for which you have been selected.

4. Congratulations!

H. A. PETREA

Congratulation letter from VFA-86 commander for my advancement.

Finally it was time for the NATO cruise. With sea bags in hands, we all arrived at the military terminal of NAS Cecil Field and waited for the flight to the homeport of our aircraft carrier, Norfolk, Virginia. We arrived in Norfolk, and a bus took us to the huge navy seaport.

All the new petty officers third class of VFA-86.

Petty Officers Creed

At Sea, on Distant Stations and at home; I will serve with Pride.

I will dedicate myself to my Country, my Shipmates and my Family.

By example I will encourage, inspire, teach, and motivate.

I will be firm, fair and consistent to those I lead.

My opportunities are unlimited.

My responsibilities are great.

I will serve God and Country with Honor and Distinction.

Here it was; the gigantic aircraft carrier stood tall in the water and waited for the sailors to arrive. It looked so massive. I couldn't believe I was actually about to step on an American aircraft carrier. The ship was named after this country—USS *America* (CV-66). It was so cool, and I was speechless, as I looked the surroundings.

USS America (CV-66).

"Don't Thread On Me"

Our squadron checked into the section designated for us. Everything here was one compartment after the other. I kept walking until I saw my tiny bed. Underneath the little cushion was my little storage. The space was really limited because thousands of sailors would be on this ship. I would be spending my resting time on this tiny bed for the next two months.

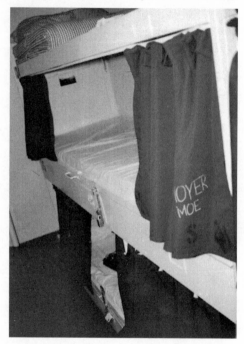

The sailor's bed.

The sailor's closet.

The ship was underway but I didn't feel the movements at all. Curious, I went to an open deck and took a look just to see if the ship was really moving. I saw a gigantic piece of steel floating on the water and heading to the open Atlantic Ocean. I just couldn't believe what I was really experiencing.

Once we'd been at sea for a few days, I'd had the chance to check out the ship entirely. The ship was just like a floating city and it had almost everything. The ship had a very large chow hall, and the food was great. I loved this area and I could eat more than three times a day if I had the chance. It also had a few retail stores and gift shops. Best of all, it had a gym for sailors who wanted to exercise in between the long hours. This would be one of my favorite places in the ship. I was skinny, and I always wanted to have a little more muscle mass on my body. I would like to build the strength of endurance so that I would be able to deal with hard and long working hours on the ship and to stay away from vulnerable sickness. I had to focus on this goal. By the time, I got off this ship in two months; I might be a few pounds heavier and a better sailor.

After several days, we had reached the frigid water of the North Atlantic and Norwegian Fjords within the Arctic Circle. Our mission was to participate in NATO exercise North Star 89. Our ship would conduct numerous hours of flight operations to prove that the United States was capable of putting an aircraft carrier anywhere and launching fighters in any unfavorable conditions from any seas around the world.

Many times, I took breaks during daylight. I stood on the balcony and looked toward the Arctic horizon. I would wonder how it was possible that I'd ended up here on the aircraft carrier. How could I imagine this in a million years? Then from a distance, I would see the snow-covered peaks of Norway's mountains that were surrounding the Vest Fjord and feel the freezing air temperature. In many ways, this created romantic pictures in my soul. My mind would suddenly recall a lot of memories from years ago.

I had lost my first love on the day I had fled my country and left behind the first girl I'd ever kissed. Standing here on an aircraft carrier in the hardy, cold weather made my heart lonesome. As a natural reflex, I called out her name. I was missing the love that I lost from the deepest of my soul. I loved her dearly and wondered what she was up to. The last time she wrote me that she was trying to escape, and then I had never heard from her again. The question was always still in my mind—had she ever escaped and made it to free land? I was here in the North Atlantic Ocean, but if I were in the Pacific Ocean, I would look down to the water more often, and perhaps I would see her boat and rescue her.

I needed to get back to my shop. We worked very hard—our shortest days were fourteen-hour long—seven days a week. We did have breaks in between, but we all were very exhausted at the end of the day and, through the exhaustion, it would make it the best medicine for everyone to have a good night sleep on our most comfortable, tiny beds every night.

Suddenly one early morning, I was awoken by a lot of noise in my rack area. I got out of my bed and asked my teammates what was going on. They told me it was time for Blue Nose Initiation. I had no clue what that was, but I figured I had to participate along with everybody else. I put on my clothes and follow the crowd to the flight deck. When I got to the deck, I couldn't believe what I saw. People were wearing weird customs and makeup. They looked very funny, but their actions were very scary. I was confused. I didn't know this could happen on a United States Aircraft Carrier, and I didn't know why it was happening.

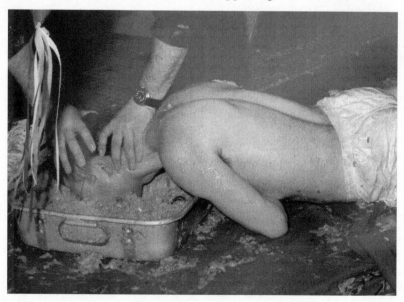

Part of the Blue Nose Initiation.

The ship was still moving at a fair speed, and with the wind blowing off the Norwegian Sea, the wind-chill factor was well below zero on the flight deck and the sailors on the ship were doing the Navy tradition of Blue Nose initiation for sailors who were crossing the North Arctic Circle for the first time. The elder made the new sailors crawl on their bellies or walk like penguins. They made fun of us in many different ways. Many of us wanted to be tough, so we took any orders and did whatever the elder shipmates wanted us to do. I knew no harm would come to this, so I didn't mind; but I hoped I would get over the Blue Nose Initiation quickly.

The good part was that once the new sailors had gained the membership and certified to be a frigid fraternity of the Blue Nose, they could do the same to new sailors for the next initiation and the Navy tradition goes on. I wasn't sure that I would be able to do that myself.

I finally made it to the big ice cubes where the last step for initiators sitting on the ice to make their buds frozen and waiting to be blessed. I sat and waited to be blessed by the Ice Men or the Ruler of the North Wind. I was freezing to death, and I couldn't wait for the ceremony to be over. Then Ice Men came to me and put blue paint on my nose, declaring, *"Now you are a Blue Nose."*

I immediately ran back to my place and took a good, hot shower. I put on a new set of clothes, crawled onto my rack, and lay down underneath my thick blanket. I tried to warm myself up before my body got sick. After a few hours, I felt much better. I would never forget this once in a lifetime event.

Blue Nose certificate.

Blue Nose certificate.

After the initiation of the Blue Nose, activities got back to normal business. The exercises for the operation were becoming heavier, and we were kept constantly occupied. We worked sixteen to seventeen hours for days like these. But it didn't matter how busy I was; all the excitement on the flight deck kept me going hour after hour.

Launching an aircraft into the air virtually without the runway by using the catapult device amazed me every single time. Even though this was the huge aircraft carrier but considering comparing the surface area of the aircraft carrier with any airport, the surface area on the carrier was fifty times smaller. The forces for those jet planes taking off and landing were tremendous. Every procedure had to be precise and accurate.

Because of such a small area, there was no room for error. If anything went wrong, the entire ship would be totally in disaster, especially when live ordinance were also on the flight deck. This made the flight deck on the aircraft carrier become the most dangerous place to work in the world.

Before the aircraft was airborne, the powerful columns of blue fire from the jet streams of the afterburners appeared right before it took off. The noise of the launchings was also incredible. Standing from a short distance of the launching aircraft, I could feel its affect all over my body. This was unbelievable force of power. I said to myself that I was witnessing the most ultimate excitements anybody could ever experience. This was why these pilots were the best of the best and this was why I dreamed of becoming one.

It even more spectacular when seeing these powerful aircrafts launch at nighttime, especially the F-14 Tomcats, which were the mightiest fighter jets in the world. During the launching, the whole area of North Atlantic Sea glowed in the nighttime, lit by the jet streams of its afterburners. Every time I witnessed a launch, every inch of my body vibrated even though I stood far away.

Launching the F-14 Tomcat at nighttime.

We'd been at sea for several weeks already, and we'd been working tirelessly day in and day out; but soon we were going to take a break. We were going to visit Saint Thomas Port in a few days, and we would have three days of liberty. We couldn't wait for the break, and we all were looking forward to having some good fun.

One early morning, the ship hit the port, and the Liberty Bell rang. I left the ship together with a few friends; we were all eager to get off the ship and explore the beautiful island of Saint Thomas. Being in one part of the world one day and on a totally different place the next made me feel a little strange. Several days ago, we had been in the frigid water, and today we were here at Saint Thomas, a tropical island with beautiful, warm, blue water and gorgeous beaches. Joining the US Navy was clearly the way to see the world.

Liberty pass for liberty calls.

The good times came to an end quickly.. The best thing was that we had all really enjoyed ourselves and relaxed after many consecutive days of working so hard. It was time for our ship to get underway and resume our normal business.

The ship was once again ready to conduct flight operations. As the ship drifted away from the island, I stood on the back of the ship and looked at the beautiful, green island.

This time reminded me of the saddest moment of my escape. After the horror of trying to load so many people on board the tiny boat in the darkness of the night, we had finally managed to get everything together and moved the boat from the shallow water to the open sea. As the sun slowly rose on the horizon, I stood on the back of my tiny boat and looked at the beautiful island of Vung Tau as my boat slowly drifted farther away. I remembered how painful it was for me to witness the terrible loss of my country and my family.

Today, I was standing on the back of an aircraft carrier, but I would never forget where I came from. The Communists created this deep wound in my heart and soul, and in those of millions of my people, and our wounds could never be healed until the shameless, brutal Communist regime no longer existed on the face of my beautiful Vietnam.

Our ship was moving at a steady pace. I went back to my shop to perform my duties. I felt there was always so much to do and learn. We had about fifteen jets for our squadron. Keeping up with all these jets was very challenging. We were fortunate to have very excellent supervisors and fine, smart sailors on our team. Their expertise and dedication really made a world of difference.

As the days went by, we were told that we would be hitting another port. This time, we'd be visiting Le Havre, France, and the capital, Paris. This was exciting. I had heard of Paris since I was little, the most attracting place that everyone wanted to see. Paris was the capital of the world in the nineteenth century.

Furthermore, there was a connection between France and Vietnam. A long time ago, the French government had dominated the country of Vietnam for a hundred years. This was why the Vietnamese traditions were somewhat influenced by French and the Capital Paris had become very popular among the Vietnamese. Even though the liberty was going to be short, I knew that I would I enjoy thoroughly because Paris was one of my favorites cities to visit.

Before we knew it, our ship was pulling alongside of Port Le Havre. Then the liberty bell rang; all the happy sailors were getting off the ship. My friend and I stayed local for the first day. We walked around and visited a few restaurants and relaxed. On the second day, we managed to take the bullet train to Paris. While sitting in the train, I could feel how fast the train was running. It was an exciting experience riding a train like this. I thought that there would be a very large distance between the two cities, but we arrived to Paris in fewer than thirty minutes. As soon as the door of the train opened, I stepped on the land and I realized I had just travelled to one of most the beautiful cities in the world.

My friends and I walked around this beautiful and magnificent city. We saw many unbelievable building and churches with glorious architecture that had been constructed more than a hundred years ago. I paid so much respect to the people of France as I looked at the magnificent designs and beautiful architectures.

We also visited the Eiffel Tower, the most popular symbol of France, and we came at the right time—the celebration of the hundred-year anniversary the tower.

As I got close to the tower, I realized how big it was. Because our time was so limited, we didn't have the opportunity to ride to the top of the tower. After many hours of walking, we were getting tired and hungry. It was time to find a good restaurant in the city of Paris. I remembered hearing about a lot of excellent Vietnamese restaurants in the city's 13th district. My friends were willing to try Vietnamese food so we took a taxi to that part of the city.

The Eiffel Tower in Paris.

When we got there, I couldn't help but to say, "Wow!" I couldn't believe how many Vietnamese restaurants there were. I thought I was in Saigon, Vietnam. It was so interesting.

Three days of fun and sightseeing came to an end abruptly. Our ship pulled out to sea, and we resumed our business. The deployment had been almost two months, so we would be heading home very soon. I had really enjoyed the cruise thus far.

I loved the Navy more than ever before. The Navy had given me some tough times as well as some good times. Through it, I had learned so much. It had trained me to become a strong human being. I had joined the US Navy in order for me to stand for my own beliefs, and I was doing just that. The Navy was the perfect place for me to pursue my goals and fulfilling my purpose.

It was April, and our ship was homebound now. I hoped the weather in Norfolk, Virginia, would not be as cold as it had been in February. In many respect, I was not so excited about going home because I had no home or family around. I wanted to make this ship my home. I thought I belonged here. I was one of the boat people. I was the man of the ocean, and I believed that was my fate.

I stood on the balcony and looked beyond the blue waters of the endless boundary of the high seas. It didn't matter where I was. The ocean connects one and all on this earth; the Atlantic or the Pacific Ocean is one-water of the universe. The ocean had always been my friend. I talked to my ocean when I felt sad, lonesome; or when I missed my family, and my beautiful country of Vietnam. I prayed that the ocean would always be calm and beautiful.

We had arrived in Norfolk on a very sunny April day. Our squadron prepared to get off the ship and fly back to Cecil Field, Florida. I was a little sad but not too worried because we would return here in a month for a much longer cruise—the Mediterranean deployment.

XVIII

We came back in the Sunshine State. I looked at the back of our hangar, and all of our Iron Hornets stood lined up in an at-ease position. They looked so awesome and magnificent. I told these beautiful birds that they'd completed a job well done and accomplished a mission. I was so happy and proud to be part of the team.

When May arrived, it was time for us to make the long deployment again. I was all ready for the six-month Mediterranean cruise. If somebody had asked me where I would want my ship to go for this coming long deployment, I would say that I wished my ship would conduct its exercises on the Pacific Ocean.

My reason was that the Vietnamese boat people were still escaping their country at this time and these desperate boat people would need their lives to be rescued in the southeast of the Pacific Ocean. If our battle group was conducting the exercises in that part of the ocean, I might get the chance to see the desperate and helpless Vietnamese boat people rescued; and seeing my own people, who had risked their lives seeking freedom—taking part in saving them from their tiny watercrafts—would be indescribably amazing experience.

We arrived at the aircraft carrier in the second week of May, and the ship was underway the next day. This was an emotional day for most of the sailors because they were going to leave behind their families and love ones for at least half of the calendar year. Before the ship left port, sailors, in formal white uniforms, stood at-ease all around the flight deck saying good-bye to families, friends and the land of our beloved country.

As the ship started moving, the song "God Bless America" played on the loudspeakers. It was a very touching moment for everyone, and I couldn't hold the tears in my eyes, although I had no family members on the port for me to say good-bye.

The ship had been out to sea for a day, and the ship crew started to welcome all of our heroic pilots from all the squadrons landed on the carrier. Seeing those beautiful and mighty birds maneuver and put their tail hooks down to catch the steel wires for landing was awesome. I kept looking up, just to wonder where the birds of my squadron were. After looking for a while, I thought I saw them. They were flying in a formation just as they were demonstrating an air show. They looked so beautiful, and I loved them.

Tomcat's tail hook landing.

Strkfitron-86 about to land on the carrier.

I believed that all the pilots and all the jets had arrived on the ship. Everything had been flawlessly executed. I was confident that we were going to have a great cruise.

But bad news were already here. I was at my shop when I heard from the loudspeakers that the ship's captain announced a serious fire had broken out in the engine room and claimed two lives. I was shocked. Silence fell over the shop. I felt very sorry for those sailors who had ultimately sacrificed their lives in the service for their country. I bowed my head and paid them the utmost respect, praying for their souls to be in Heaven with God. I couldn't believe it was only our third day at sea and an accident like this had happened. I prayed for the safety of our cruise every day until the end of this deployment.

Coincidently with the tragedies of our ship, I saw the *Navy Times* magazine lying on the desk in our shop. I picked up and read the issue. There, I found another tragic event; a battleship in Iowa had exploded, and forty-seven sailors had lost their lives. Among them was a Vietnamese born petty officer third class, Fire Controlman Tung Thanh Adams.

Oh my God! So many sailors died! I cried out loudly from my soul. I couldn't believe I'd received two tragic pieces of news in the same day. I wanted to give my deepest sympathy from the bottom of my heart to Tung's adoptive father, Alvin Adams, and to the families of all the other sailors who had sacrificed their lives.

140

I was already starting to feel the heat of the flight operations. We worked very hard to keep our jets in the air. This was nothing new, as this was how we'd worked during the NATO cruise. Whenever I had breaks, I chose a very good spot on the balcony so I could look far beyond the horizon. Many times I saw our battle group ships surrounding our aircraft carrier. They all looked so great and mighty. I called this the American super power; it was so great to see such strength of the United States Navy.

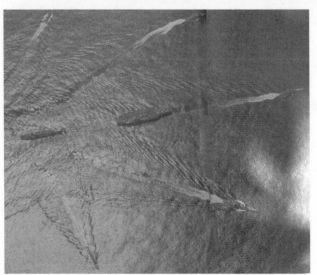

The America's team

We had been at sea for a few weeks now, and our first port visit was scheduled. In fact, we would have port visits back to back for the next four weeks. Our first port would be Benidorm, one of Spain's beautiful coastal cities. We would have six days of liberty here; a lot of time to explore this gorgeous city.

The water and beaches in Benidorm were great and the people seemed very nice and friendly. I also loved the food. It was different from what we had in our chow hall.

Replenishing fuel.

Several days after Benidorm, we visited a beautiful island in Spain called Palma. This huge island sat in the middle of the Balearic Sea. Once again, we got to see new, beautiful places. Glorious architecture made this city spectacular—too much to see it all. Besides sightseeing, my next favorite thing to do was to enjoy Spanish food. I ate too much.

After several days in Palma, our ship pulled out and headed east to the Mediterranean Sea. The flight operations resumed, and we got into to our serious business. One day, I noticed that the flight operation had stopped and our carrier had slowed down; I saw a cargo ship approaching our ship. I realized that it was time for the ship to replenish the ship's supply. I was amazed of how well the operation was carried out.

Some days, there was not much activity and the work forces had been at ease somewhat, especially the stress and pressure from those pilots who had the most responsibilities. I always respected and admired them and thanked them for their intelligence, dedication and their remarkable service to their country. Every now and then, we had short working days, and I saw our pilots walking around and relaxing. Many of them walked on the flight deck catching fresh air and probably thinking about their families and loved ones, whom they had been far apart far apart from for a while now. We all had personal moments, and I wished peace would always be with us all.

A beautiful sunset and a pilot at sea.

The construction of The Great Theatre, which seated 25,000, was completed in AD 54.

We would be making another port visit in a few days. This time we would be visiting Izmir, Turkey. I had never thought that I would see Turkey. I never knew how many adventures I was going to have when I was in the Navy. Seeing the people and the country of Turkey, where the East met the West would be so interesting.

When the ship arrived at the port of Izmir, I was eager to get off the ship. There was so much history here and so many historic places that I longed to see. I also saw statues and broken buildings of precious stones that had been built many centuries ago. The Mother of Virgin Mary's house was also believed to be in this area. It was a lot to learn from this country.

Liberty time was over, and our ship pulled out to sea. I noticed that no flight operation in the next a few days because we were heading to the Suez Canal. This was interesting news. I remembered that, when I was only in fifth grade in a school in my village in Vietnam, I had first learned about the Suez Canal during world history class. Today I was going see the canal for myself. This was really unbelievable. I would never have expected this in a million years.

The Suez Canal, located in Egypt, is over a hundred miles long. It connects the Mediterranean Sea with the Gulf of Suez. The Suez Canal was completed and opened in 1869. The construction of the canal took ten years. It had become the most popular man-made canal in the world. As the ship slipped through the narrow vein of water, I could see the sands that stretched to the horizon. I saw the Egyptians, who were standing close by the canal, waving at us. In the meantime, on the flight deck, our crewmembers took this rare opportunity to convert the flight deck into a big gym. Sailors started to run, walk, or lift weights. It was definitely an interesting and fun event for me.

Transiting through the Suez Canal.

Yesterday, we had been in the Mediterranean Sea, and today, we were in the Arabian Sea. After a day of Suez Canal transit, we were now conducting exercises with the Saudi Arabian forces. The flight operations resumed, and we were getting busy. However, my squadron had temporarily assigned me a special duty when some departments of the ship didn't have enough personnel. I was sent to office of the master-at-arms to be a part of the team charged with keeping peace and order inside our ship. This would be totally a different task. My job was to patrol a certain section of the ship and get involved in, solve, and report any violence or disorderly conduct of any sailor to a higher authority. I took the new order as a new challenge for me.

Master-at-Arms Petty Officer Du T. Hua.

Things were going smoothly so far. The month of July was almost here, and the birthday of the United States of America was coming. This would be my first time celebrating the biggest national holiday on the ship that carried the country's name. We were going to glorify the birthday of America two days shy of the actual date because of the busy operation schedules.

On the morning of July 2, 1989, one of my favorite songs, "America the Beautiful" poured from the loudspeakers I stood on the balcony in the middle of the high sea under a beautiful sky and listened to every word of the song and every note of the music:

O Beautiful for spacious skies...

America, America, God shed his grace on thee.

And crown thy good with brotherhood from sea to shining sea."

America, America—it was my home—the home of the free.

The noise started to get louder and the flight deck had soon transformed into a huge outdoor picnic. We called this Steel Beach BBQ. My friends and I stood in line for hot, juicy real American hamburgers and hot dogs.

Steel beach BBQ.

Sharing America's Birthday cake.

At the end of the day, our celebration of the birthday of the nation came to an end; glorifying the holiday like this had boosted the morale and spirit of our sailors. I loved this country more than ever. I was very thankful to live in freedom and democracy. Nothing was more precious than that.

I patrolled the ship as it was underway for flight operations. I worked a shorter hour schedule at the master-at-arms office, so I had more time to go to the gym. I was in better shape than before. Through a combination of good food and exercise, I had gained some muscle mass, and I felt stronger and healthier. I was very happy and proud of myself.

*Pollywogs crawling up
to the ceremony.*

One early morning, I heard a lot of noise, and my shipmates were running up to the flight deck. I got out of my rack and asked my teammate what were going on. He told me it was the Cross the Line initiation. I had no idea what that was or why someone had to go through that. Nobody had the chance to explain, but one of my teammates told me that if I didn't want to go, I should just stay in my rack.

I certainly didn't want to stay in my rack because my ego and curiosity were bigger than that. I followed the others up to the deck; I wanted to be part of it even though I had no clue what was happening and why. When I approached the flight deck, people started calling me pollywog, and they called themselves the trusty shellback or the sons of Neptune. They made me crawl on the flight deck to the places of the initiation. Messy food and nasty liquids in different kinds were everywhere. All forms of making fun of the Pollywogs who were the first time crossed the line. I realized that this was just another Navy tradition—whenever the ship was crossing the equator, a ceremony was held to initiate new sailors and make them tougher and fully, 100 percent sailor proof. Seeing my fellow sailors in weird costumes and makeup was very funny. All the shellbacks were having too much fun to make the pollywogs suffer. It was very tough, and that was the name of the game. This was my second initiation, so I was fully aware what I needed to do to become tougher and get through this. My group and I finally got the declaration from the king of Neptune. *"I do hereby command all hands to honor and respect him as a trusty shellback."* I did it, and I was tough.

Crossing The Line   July 12, 1989

Time to hear the command from the king of Neptune.

Shell back certificate.

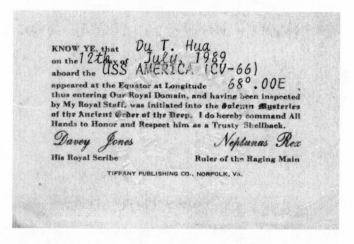

Things were getting back to normal quickly. I had now completed my temporary duty as a master-at-arms, and returned to my squadron. I was glad because I had been missing the works on my airplanes.

The ship was now in the Indian Ocean and conducting heavy flight operations. Whenever I could, I went to the newsroom to check out some Navy magazines, so that I could keep up with what was going on in the Navy. Indeed, I caught some interesting news that made me really excited. An article in *All Hands Magazines* reported that the USS *Oldendorf* had rescued thirty-five Vietnamese boat people from their tiny vessel in the Gulf of Thailand. Involved in the rescue was a Vietnamese sailor, Khoi Thanh Nguyen, who was stationed on *Oldendorf*. Khoi, who was once a refugee and had been rescued by the US Navy in 1975 after the Fall of Saigon. Khoi was able to immediately connect with the refugees and help them in the rescue process. I felt great and so happy that God had blessed the people who had just been saved. I wished I could have the same opportunity like Khoi. That would be the greatest feeling; but my ship was now in the Indian Ocean; there was no way any refugee boat would be drifting this way.

Rescue at sea

USS Oldendorf *pulls 35 Vietnamese refugees from the Gulf of Thailand.*

Story and photos by JO1 Patrick E. Winter

The destroyer USS *Oldendorf* (DD 972) recently sailed into Subic Bay, Republic of the Philippines, carrying 35 Vietnamese refugees picked up in the Gulf of Thailand, about 60 miles southwest of the southern tip of Vietnam.

For one of the *Oldendorf* crew, Seaman Khoi Dinh Nguyen, an operations specialist, the rescue brought back memories of when he himself was a refugee. "It's been a long time," Nguyen said. "I left Vietnam in 1975, when I was only six years old. I was really happy to have a chance to help.

"I was up in the combat information center at the time the Vietnamese were sighted," Nguyen said. "When we took our small boat up to their vessel, they all started talking to me at once," said Nguyen, a Wichita, Kan., resident.

Nguyen was instrumental to the rescue's success according to LCDR William Smart, *Oldendorf's* executive officer. "Nguyen, the squadron medical officer and I were in the boarding party. As it turned out, some of the refugees had the same last name as Nguyen. They immediately established a rapport once they learned that he was a former refugee himself. The Vietnamese remained calm and cooperated very well with Nguyen — they were perfect guests."

"The rest of the crew helped out a lot," Nguyen said. "They donated clothes and other odds and ends for all the refugees."

Once in port, the Vietnamese were taken to a United Nations refugee camp by U.N. representatives, to begin the immigration process.

For the crew of *Oldendorf*, forward-deployed to Yokuska, the rescue meant a couple of days liberty in the Philippines before heading back to sea. But for Nguyen, the experience had a deeper meaning: it reminded him why he was on the rescue ship.

"I joined the Navy partly because I was young and wanted to have fun," he said, "and partly because I was rescued by a U.S. Navy warship and I just wanted to see what it was like on the other side." □

Winter is assigned to the Public Affairs Rep., 7th Fleet, Subic Bay, Republic of the Philippines.

Sailor Nguyen helps refugees filling out paperworks.

Preceding page: Nguyen helps a family fill out paper work. Left: An elderly woman prepares for the trip to the Philippines. Top: Petty Officer 1st Class Joaquin Joubert joins the youngsters in an electronic game. Above: Things are looking brighter for this young refugee in the arms of Petty Officer Gerome Baldwin.

Refugees settling on the rescuing ship.

After reading that article, images of desperate, helpless faces of the boat people I had known – had been one of – played often in my mind. I remembered my own rescue and thanked God again for our angel, the Cap Anamur. I knew that those people had truly been willing to make the ultimate sacrifice for freedom and dignity.

Our ship was moved at a steady pace, and the flight operations got heavier in the Indian Ocean. My teammates and I were busy maintaining our airplanes. We sometimes cracked jokes and made fun of each other just to make our work more pleasurable.

One day, a teammate told me that he couldn't wait for the Singapore port visit. I was stunned. I asked him to repeat himself. *"Are you sure we are going to Singapore?"*

He said yes, noting that he'd seen the new schedule. I immediately ran to the shop and asked my supervisor, just to confirm that it was true. It was true, indeed. Our ship was going to hit Singapore port in just a few more days. I was extremely happy and excited, not because I wanted to see Singapore but because I thought our ship might have the chance to rescue the Vietnamese boat people in the South China Sea in the Pacific Ocean— the waters near Singapore, Malaysia, Thailand, and the Philippines.

I started counting the days until our ship would head to Singapore. I also wanted to know when our ship would be in the Pacific Ocean. By looking at the schedule, I figured that, in one more day, my ship would be out of the Indian Ocean and in the Pacific Ocean.

I continued to read a lot of news in the Navy magazines. I kept searching for news of any more boat people being rescued. Surprisingly, I read another good bit of news about the refugees. This news came from the Transitions Navy Magazine under *Refugees Rescued at Sea*. A frigate, the USS *Kirk* (FF-1087) had spotted a refugee boat with nine people on board in the South China Sea. The boat people were surprised when, from the Navy ship, someone spoke down to them in their native language. Wow! How could that be? They were astonished to learn that, on the frigate *Kirk*, there was a former Vietnamese refugee just turned US sailor several months earlier. Fireman Apprentice Long T. Huynh had escaped from Vietnam nine years earlier and, interestingly, had been rescued by the US Navy. After graduating from high school in San Diego, Long had joined US Navy and been stationed on the frigate *Kirk*. How cool was that!

I was very happy for those nine boat people. Their lives had been saved, and now they had their freedom in their hands. I was also very happy for Long who had had the opportunity to save his own people. I wanted to congratulate him. From my own aircraft carrier, I prayed that God would give me the same opportunity to save my own poor people.

Transitions

Refugee turned sailor: Once a refugee boat occupant himself, Fireman Apprentice Long Huynh, a 1985 graduate of W.C. Overfelt High School in San Jose, Calif., was instrumental in the rescue of nine Vietnamese refugees in the South China Sea.

Fireman Apprentice Long T. Huynh with his frigate, the USS Kirk.

Refugees rescued at sea

SOUTH CHINA SEA — When frigate Kirk (FF-1087) pulled up alongside a fishing boat displaying an SOS sign in international waters recently, the men aboard the boat were relieved to see the American flag flying from Kirk's mast.

More so, the nine Vietnamese men were surprised to hear someone speaking to them in their native language from Kirk's decks.

The voice belonged to Fireman Apprentice Long T. Huynh, a former Vietnamese refugee himself, who recently joined the U.S. Navy.

"When our ship came alongside the refugees' boat, it took me back nine years ago to when I escaped the same way," the 21-year-old Huynh said.

Huynh's boat was intercepted in international waters by a U.S. Navy ship, which transported the refugees to a camp in Malaysia. Huynh and his friends were later transferred to a camp in the Philippines before emigrating to the United States.

In the recent encounter, Kirk was returning from a port visit in Thailand when a boat of refugees from Vietnam was spotted. Huynh joined the rescue team and established communications.

The refugees were taken by Kirk to Subic Bay, Philippines, where they were processed by United Nations officials and taken to the Morong Bataan refugee camp.

Huynh reported aboard Kirk in April, after graduating from the Navy's basic boiler technician school in San Diego.

Rescuing news.

My teammate and I went up to the flight deck to work on a minor problem on one of our Hornets. Walking on the flight deck during operations was extremely dangerous. I had to walk around the A-6s (attack jets) that already had their engines running. I passed in front of their intakes, and even though I wasn't too close, I felt the power as the intakes sucked in air, pulled by the powerful force, I almost lost my balance. A shipmate who was nearby reached out his hand and pulled me back. He may have saved me from being swallowed into the intake of the A-6. If that had happened, my entire body would have become burger meat. I thanked him for watching out for his shipmate, and I promised him I would be extremely careful around the areas.

While we were fixing the minor problem on the Hornet, I watched the other Hornets being launched. There was nothing cooler than to see the catapult shooting the jet into the air.

A Hornet being shot into the air by a catapult.

154

One next day I arose very early the next morning. I didn't know how far we were from Singapore, but I knew for sure that we were in the Pacific Ocean now. I put on my working uniform and walked toward my shop. First, I stood on a balcony and looked down to the water. I wondered if today would be the day I might see a refugee boat.

I couldn't stand on the balcony for long. I needed to go to my shop before I was late for work. When I arrived at the shop, I started working just like any other normal working day. However, Every couple of hours, I took a break and went to the balcony to look down at the water below me and far beyond. I prayed to God—if any refugee boats were in the area, please let us rescue them before they die.

I then thought of my girlfriend. She had told me that she was going to escape, but I had never heard anything from her. Could today be the day I might see? Could hers be the boat we rescued? I shook my head. It was impossible.

My first love,
Phan Nguyệt Ánh.

Even so, I still wanted to see that dream to come true. Oh my God! How wonderful that would be. I still missed her. I still thought of our time together and I remembered every time we dated. The love I gave to her was natural, and my love for my first love came from deep within me. I opened my wallet and took out the little picture of her face that she gave to me at a time when we were deeply in love. I had it with me at all time lately. I asked myself whether there was any chance that my ship would rescue her boat on our way to Singapore. Once again, I shook my head and pushed all of those feelings away. I didn't want to raise hope in myself and feel the disappointment and pain in my heart and soul if that didn't happen. I needed to stop thinking and get back to my shop.

I looked down to the water several times throughout the day. I still saw nothing but dark blue ocean. I figured I was setting myself up for disappointment, but I didn't give up yet. Our ship would still be in this part of the ocean for several days.

It was a long day at work, and my energy ran completely out. I was exhausted. I needed to hit my rack badly.

Aviation Machinist Mate team of VFA-86.

After taking a shower, I crawled onto my bed and lay down with my comfortable pillow. My body and mind were out before I even realized it. But, somehow, I thought I saw a very bad storm with very dark clouds coming. The face of the ocean turned violent, and one big wave came after another. Through the frightening scene, I spotted a tiny refugee vessel crowded with children. Oh my God! I screamed out to the captain of our ship, begging him to rescue the people before the boat capsized.

Suddenly, among the refugees in the boat, I saw my girlfriend. She stood up, called my name, and extended her hand out, asking for my help.

"Please wait," I called. *"I'm coming to rescue you."*

Then from out of nowhere, a huge wave came and slammed over her boat, creating a terrifying noise.

I sat up quickly, hitting my head very hard against the rack above in the tight space. My shipmate explained that he'd knocked on my rack loudly to wake me up because he'd heard me mumbling so much in my sleep. He checked on me and wondered if I was okay.

My eyes now were opened, but I was breathing very heavily. After a few minutes, I felt okay. I told my shipmate I was all right; it was just a very bad dream. I thanked him for checking on me and wished him a good night of sleep.

Back at work the next day, the horrible dream remained with me vividly. I wanted to share my dream with my teammates, but on second thought, I didn't. I was afraid they might make fun of me. I decided to keep it to myself. I tried to focus on my work normally. However, I continued to run back and forth to the balcony to look down at the water. The ship now was very close to Singapore. Tomorrow we were going to hit the port of this beautiful city; but my mind was not on the liberty call at this time.

We arrived in Singapore. I saw so many ships floating on this huge area of the blue water making a beautiful scene. Our ship was anchored in the middle of the water and we had to take a ferryboat to go to shore.

Singapore was a beautiful and interesting port, and my friends couldn't stop talking about this port visit. They all were looking forward to have the best time in this sensational city.

Although my mind wasn't ready for this liberty call, I got to see this Lion City. I had never been here before, but a lot of Vietnamese boat people had escaped to this country and stayed here for a while before settling in their third country. I wanted to go and see the Vietnamese refugee camp that I knew was somewhere in this country. I asked some of the local people, and no one knew where it was.

Singapore was a very clean and beautiful city. I went to a huge outdoor market. Everything looked similar to the market in Saigon. I bought a lot of tropical fruits because these fruits were the same fruits in Vietnam and I certainly missed eating them.. It was time for me to enjoy these fruits. I asked my friends to share with me and they also loved them.

Suddenly, our ship had an order to pull out early due to an emergency situation arising from the Desert Storm Operation of the Persian War. The captain had cancelled the remaining days of the liberty calls and ordered all hands back to their stations. I had intended to make a better effort and find the Vietnamese refugee center, but since we pulled out early, I had to miss my chance. It was okay; when I heard of the emergency situation, I thought of my ship, and my country came first. I was happy to return to my ship.

My ship started heading out of the Pacific Ocean. I still watched the water, searching and scouting for any refugees boats, but I saw nothing. It was time to move on, and I wanted to get my mind settled so I could focus on my important work in my shop. Our ship was rushing to the Persian Gulf areas for a great cause.

The flight operations were so heavy that we were working very long days and nights. We were in this area for a few weeks and working intensively.

During one lunch break, I was reading a *Navy Times* magazine. I saw more good news for the Vietnamese refugees. The USS *Dubuque* had just rescued thirty boat people on a very small watercraft. The ship's captain had decided to launch the rescue because he realized that the refugees' vessel was not seaworthy and overloaded with a lot of refugees on board. The tiny watercraft was spotted four hundred nautical miles from Singapore on August 13. Wow! My ship had been in the area about ten days ago. I told myself that I might have seen that refugee boat.

USS Dubuque rescues 30 refugees

In the early morning hours of August 13, USS Dubuque (LPD-8) rescued 30 Vietnamese refugees from a small boat in the South China Sea.

The Dubuque was about 400 nautical miles away from their ultimate destination of Singapore when they spotted the overloaded 35-foot craft.

The refugees, 23 adults and seven children, boarded Dubuque after an inspection determined their vessel was unseaworthy.

Medical personnel examined the the refugees and treated some for dehydration. The refugees were then transported to Singapore for further transfer.

Dubuque is an Amphibious Transport Dock ship homeported in Sasebo, Japan and commanded by Capt. D.L. Wetherell.

Rescuing news.

After several intense weeks of flight operations in the Persian Gulf, we headed back to the Gulf of Suez, transiting through the Suez Canal to the Mediterranean Sea. We would soon make another port visit, this one in Toulon, France. I was sure that everyone needed a break this time.

We arrived in Toulon during the second week of September. We would spend five days here for liberty calls. Toulon was another beautiful city, with gorgeous long beaches. I had a chance to catch a bus to another beautiful nearby city, Nice. What stunning views I found there; I had never seen the beach like this before. There was no sand, but the beach was covered with pretty stones or gravel. I was glad I had my camera with me.

A knockout sunset in the gorgeous city of Nice, France.

The very nice break came to an end, and we got back to the waters and resumed our operations. Thus far, we had been deployed for about four months. The routines had become very familiar, but most of the sailors were missing their loved ones very much. One of my teammates told me that he couldn't wait to return home to see his girlfriend. I told him that I very much understood his situation and asked him to just hang in there; we were coming to the last part of the cruise, and we would be home before we knew it.

He asked me if I had a girlfriend, and I told him that I didn't but that I had been looking for one all over the Pacific Ocean when our ship had been approaching Singapore. He didn't seem to understand, so I had to

159

tell him a little more about what had happened to me and to my first love. I even told him that I still loved her and dreamed about her. I also told him about the nightmare I'd had. He was the one who had checked on me that night.

His eyes grew wide as I quickly summarized my love story. "Wow!" he replied. He told me he couldn't believe how much I had gone through.

After the conversation, we understood each other a little more. We shook hands, and I thanked him for listening. Then we got back to work.

I kept collecting and reading news from the Navy magazines. In *The Airwinger Navy News*, I read about a guided missile cruiser, the USS *Vincennes*, which had just rescued twenty-six boat people in the South China Sea last week. I couldn't believe that this tiny vessel had been floating in the high seas for fifteen days with barely any food or water during the last days of drifting and nobody had died. This was unbelievable news for the Vietnamese refugee community.

After fifteen long years since the Fall of Saigon, the people of South Vietnam were still fleeing from the Communist regime in search of freedom and democracy. These stories were proof that the dictatorship and brutality were far beyond what the innocent people of Vietnam should or would endure. So many people were willing to die if they could not live free. These boat people knew their simple watercrafts were not seaworthy, but they took the huge risk. Tragically, only a fraction of these people made it to freedom.

Rescuing news.

October was here, and the end of our six-month cruise was nearing. But we continued to work tirelessly. My favorite thing to do on the aircraft carrier whenever I had a break was to enjoy the excitement of the launchings and landings of the fighter jets. I hoped that, some day, I would be the one sitting in the cockpit and flying one of these powerful jets. That was still my dream, and even though I knew making it come true would be a very long road, I hoped I could continue to keep my dream alive.

A nice picture of a Tomcat getting ready for launching.

We would be hitting another French port, Monaco, in a few days. We arrived at the port on a beautiful, sunny morning. This famous French city had one of the most attractive coastlines, along with imperial architecture—magnificent buildings, museums, and hotels. Things were very pricey here, so every sailor's wallet would be empty by the time we left, especially we were going to stay here for several days.

After having plenty of fun and rest for several days in Monaco, we would pull out to sea again. Surprisingly, we would be revisiting Palma, Spain, the very next day. In my understanding, this second stop was, in part, to replenish the ship's supplies. After relaxing for a few more days, we pulled out to sea and headed westward.

We were soon moving back to sea, and I believed we had done all the port visits for the deployment. November was just around the corner, and the day to go home was near. We didn't have a lot of flight operations anymore, but every now and then, I saw a few. We took it easy, biding our time until we came back home. Many of the sailors couldn't wait to see their families and friends. I knew they were counting down the days. I could see so much happiness coming to all of the sailors and their families at the end of the cruise. I was very happy for them; their families and loved ones would be together again, and I wished that they would all enjoy every single moment of the homecoming and the reunions with their families.

When we were almost home—only half a day away from Norfolk homeport. All of our airplanes had flown off the ship and the atmosphere was totally different now. Everyone was anxiously waiting to come home. Music played over the loudspeakers. One of the songs I liked most was "Coming to America" by Neil Diamond. That's right. It's time to come to America, the country I loved and adored.

I could see the city of Norfolk on the horizon. It was the second week of November. The sailors who were stationed on the ship were standing all around the flight deck in formal blue uniforms. They looked awesome. I wished I could stand there with them and look down at the spectators at the port—showing a great feeling of pride for a job well done. The ship was very close to the port now, and it was moving very slowly. I could see the huge crowd. I even saw a huge welcome home sign from a distance. I couldn't imagine how much love and support the sailors had from their families and friends. It would be so wonderful to see loved ones waiting on the port when the ship returned after such a long deployment.

As we walked off the ship, the crowd grew even larger. All the people surrounding me were kissing, hugging, laughing, crying, talking, smiling, and yelling. In this crowd, I could see the greatest happiness that I had ever seen in my life. I was truly happy for my shipmates. By not expecting anyone, I carried my heavy sea-bag and walked myself to the bus.

What a great crowd.

Welcome home America.

I got onto the bus along with a few of my teammates. The bus would be here for a while before taking off to the airport. As I sat on the bus and watched the crowd, I wished my family, especially my parents, were here. Anytime there was an event like this, I missed my parents deeply in my heart and soul. I hadn't heard anything from them lately. I wondered how they were doing. They were getting older every day, and my soul cried when I thought about not having seen them for so many years.

Finally all of my teammates were on the bus, and we headed to the base airport to fly back to our home base NAS Cecil Field, Florida.

When we arrived in Florida, we had a few days off before getting everything back together and resuming our normal business on land. The holiday season was just around the corner, and I requested my vacation during Christmas time.

I flew to Houston to spend the holidays with my brother's family. I really missed my nephew and nieces. I had good times every time I was home to visit.

After a short vacation, I flew back to Florida to my squadron. It's time to get busy.

During this time, I had a few friends outside of the base. They asked me if I wanted to move out of my barracks in the Navy base and be their roommate in a nice, nearby apartment. I thought that would be a great idea. It would give me a little more freedom and relaxation, as well as increase my social activities, which was, perhaps, what I needed most. I wanted to expand my comfort zone and be able to enjoy life a little more. I joined my friends and moved into an apartment—just my sea bag and me.

When I first moved into the new apartment, my room looked very empty, since I hadn't had a chance to buy any furniture at all. I had only a comforter and a pillow on the carpet floor for my bed with a telephone set in the corner of the room.

One evening I came home from work, and I was very tired. All I wanted to do was get some sleep before the next working day. It was very late at night when my phone rang. Worn out, I lay on the carpet in the dark room wondering who was calling me. I reluctantly picked up the phone. It was my brother, and he broke the worst news I could ever imagine. Our father had just passed away a few days ago in Vietnam. My world was shattered. My heart was broken. My brother and I just cried on our phones, unable to say anything. In the end, I could only say a few words. *"What am I going to do now?"* I asked.

My father.

XIX

My father died at the worst possible time. I had always carried with me the hope that I could see him one day and we could go on vacation to see places. I hadn't had a chance to show my father my love and care. When I was little, I was under his watch. When I was growing up, he was barely around me because of the war and the Communists. When I was fully grown, we lived on different sides of the ocean. What pained me the most was that I couldn't even fly home to say good-bye to my father for the last time. I couldn't even attend my own father's funeral.

I was in so much pain over the next several days, and I didn't know what to do. I spoke with my brother several times. All we could do was to comfort each other and pray very hard for my father's soul to go to Heaven. Days like these were so unbearable.

I tried to stand up with a lot of pain in my soul. I was sure that my father would want me to go on. He understood that we had been through times that were both difficult and gruesome, and I knew that he always wanted me to have the best possible future and freedom in my hands. I needed to keep moving and make my father, who was now in Heaven, proud.

I needed to get back to work. It was very hard thinking that my father had gone and I no longer had hope of seeing him ever again. I was depressed because there was nothing I could do. I had to accept the facts that we all were in God's hands. I needed to get myself functioning again.

Several days later, I felt much better. I found a Buddhist Temple in the Jacksonville area. I went there and prayed for my father several times. I thought this was the least I could do. The healing process began and I prayed to God to grant me peace so that I could stay strong.

But in the coming days, I found myself walking under the darkest cloud of my life. My brother in Houston called me and broke out another piece of bad news. My second brother had gotten very ill and been admitted to an intensive care unit in Saigon.

Then a few days later, I received the worst possible news--my second brother also had just died.

I stayed in my dark room, and I cried out loudly from the top of my lungs. "Why! Why! Why! What is happening to me and to my family?"

My second brother was only thirty-five years old. I had so much hope for him because he was young and intelligent. I had planned that, one day, we would meet together and guide our big families to carry out the good name for our family's next generation. He was the only son of my parents who had stayed in the homeland and taken care of the family business. Worse, he had three children of his own, and the youngest was just over a year old. Now all of his small children were fatherless. How much more painful could this be? How would his wife survive with three young children? I couldn't cry loudly enough; I couldn't cry long enough. My heart had shattered, and my soul had broken in pieces. I had lost two family members in such a short period of time. How could I survive this? I didn't even have anyone nearby to talk to. My mind could only see the dolefulness around me.

My second brother.

I really needed to be calm. Whatever it was I was facing, I had no choice but to get through it. My father and my brother didn't want to see me collapse. I needed to reinforce my strength and stand up again. I knew their souls watched over me and would help me go through this horrible time. I had a job to do and a duty to perform, so I prayed very hard for them to lead and guide me.

How could anyone imagine the pain I suffered internally? I wouldn't wish this upon to anybody. I slowly gathered my energy and determination. I had a purpose to pursue. I had missions to accomplish. I could not stop. I needed to exert all of my power mentally and physically so I could walk and function like a normal person once again.

I had finally got back to my well-being. I went to work every day with a lot of memories of my father and brother on my mind.

I stayed busy with my squadron every day. I also managed to go to school in the evenings after work if I could. I started taking a few college classes, such as American history and English composition, on the Navy Base. I figured if I kept doing this, I would attain my bachelor's degree one day. I had also applied for my American citizenship, now that I had lived in this country for more than five years already. I thought that, if I became an American citizen and had a Bachelor's degree in my hand, I would be able to apply for the Navy's officer candidate program. I was very excited about my long-term plan. If I became a Navy officer, I would be able to serve this country more than I dreamed.

One morning, I arrived at work along with my teammates. We received an order from our supervisor to take many of the external tanks off the aircrafts. We—the five of us altogether—took the order and headed out to get the work done. One of my teammate had the tool to unlock the mounting, and two of us locked our arms in place at each end of the external tank so we could bring the tank down slowly and put it onto the pulling cart.

The most crucial step we needed to take was to read inside the external tank to check the fuel level. If the tank was not empty, we should not remove it. So my teammate, the one who had the tool to unlock the mounting, opened the tank's cap and checked. After taking the reading, my teammate declared that the tank was empty and gave us a thumbs-up.

Two of us had our arms locked on each end of the tank, and we gave the signal for my teammate to unlock the mounting. As soon as my teammate unlocked the mounting, the tank, with our arms still locked around it, slammed onto the deck; four of us went down with the fully loaded fuel tank that contained hundreds of gallons. I heard something pop in my back; I knew something was wrong. Out of the four of us, I was the smallest guy. My weakness might put more pressure on my body; but I seemed okay at that time. My teammates asked me if I was all right to go on and take other tanks off. Even though I had a little bit of a strange feeling in my back, I told them I was all right to move on and get the job done. We went on and took several other tanks off after that.

I went home after that long day of work. I started feeling some discomfort in my back and put a heating pack on my lower back. Over the next several days, the pain in my lower back radiated down to my right leg and it was unbearable.

Oh my God! What was happening to me now! The pain was getting more and more severe every day. I thought this was just minor and would go away in a few days. I didn't understand, and I refused to say that there was something wrong with my back and leg. I tried to ignore the pain and continued going to work. Some of the movements made the pain manageable, but others were excruciating. Part of the job was to dive deep into the intakes and inspect all the rotor blades and make sure they were okay before the pilot started the jet engines. Diving into the intake caused the worst pain. Because I wanted to say there was nothing wrong with me, I had to block out the pain mentally and get the jobs done. That caused a great deal of suffering. I kept doing that for a few days; but soon, I could no longer deny the pain. I finally got permission from my supervisor to go to the sick hall and get checked out.

I couldn't believe it when I realized that the accident during the removal of the external tank had caused me a very bad injury on my lower back. The MRI imaging showed slipped discs in my lower back between L4-L5 and L5-S1 of the lumbar region; the region had become herniated by the sudden heavy force. Since the discs had become herniated, they had pinched the nerve roots, which had caused my right leg to become weak, heavy, numb, and painful. This horrible news blew me away. This injury was going to affect my life tremendously. What in the world had happened to me?

As a result of the excruciating pain, I was assigned to limited duty. I was very depressed because I couldn't do my regular work anymore until I became fit for duty again. My life had fallen into another pitfall. I didn't know what else to do but to fight back. This time was even more serious because it was my health, my body. I wouldn't surrender; I was a fighter. I had to step back and figure out a plan to deal with my situation.

Over the following several weeks, I followed every step my orthopedic doctors and neurosurgeons recommended. I started physical therapies, used medications, and did my basic exercises every morning. The majority of the drugs were for alleviating pain, nonsteroidal anti-inflammatory medications, and I was taking them up to three to four times daily. The drugs helped kill a great deal of the pain, but it kept coming back.

My doctors even offered me epidural steroid injections for my lower back. Although the prognosis was only temporary, I had to go through a painful process to receive the injections.

After a few months of medications and physical therapy, my doctors wanted another set of MRI images. The imaging didn't show any difference. The slipped disc in my lower back had stayed the same. My neurosurgeon now offered me the last option—surgery. During the surgery, the surgeon would cut my back open, go through my spine at the lumbar region, and fix the slip discs. I asked my neurosurgeon what the prognosis of surgery would be. He couldn't tell me clearly. All he could say was the prognosis might not be very high. In some cases, the pain might not go away and the situation might get worse. He asked me to think about it and let him know.

The idea of surgery stayed in my mind for the following several weeks. I didn't know what to do. My Navy career was about to slip out of my hands. My dreams were about to be shattered. I had never thought something like this would happen to me. Now it came down to the toughest decision of my life. Would I take the chance to gamble and put my spine and my health on the line? I contemplated the vital and crucial roles of the spine—the most important structure of the bones that controlled our critical movements. And full recovery was not guaranteed. I became very depressed; feeling like my life was about to fall apart.

As I dealt with the excruciating pain, I was working in a limited duty in a computer operation unit in NAS Jacksonville. I missed my regular job. I couldn't see the excitement of the flight operation any more. I missed repairing and maintaining the F/A-18 engines. The more I thought about it, the more depressed I became. Many times, I felt very lonesome because I didn't have anybody to talk to or to share thoughts/feelings with. My feeling was down.

One day I was very happy to meet a few new friends in the local area. One of my friends had a wife who had just given birth to a baby at the local hospital and who didn't understand English at that time. My friend told me that his wife had received help from a medical technologist intern in the hospital. This intern, who understood Vietnamese, had translated for his wife and she gave his wife her telephone number just in case his wife had any questions. I told my friend that the intern must be a very nice person, as she was willing to go that far to help another person. I asked my friend if he could introduce me to the intern the next time he had an opportunity.

Indeed, by a mutual arrangement, my friend was talking with the intern while I was with him one day. I asked my friend if I could just say hello to her after he was done talking with her. My friend gave me his phone, and I said hello to this nice intern. I asked her if I could call her next time just to make friend. She welcomed my idea.

I called and talked with her several times. She sounded very sweet on the phone, and she seemed to be a hardworking, ethical person. She had also escaped the Communist regime, traveling with her aunt and her brother in 1979 from Vietnam. Her father, who belonged to the former South Vietnamese Navy, had also escaped. But the Vietcong had caught him and put him in the hard cell prison. Her father had been brave, and showing no fear for the Communists, he had escaped from the prison and made another escape by boat out of Vietnam. The second time, he made it successfully. After the intern told me that, I had so much respect for her father.

We talked numerous times and became friends, although we hadn't seen each other yet. Many times I told her I'd like to meet her and invited her to dinner, but she refused because she had to study and prepare for her state board exam in medical technology. I respected that, and I waited for the next opportunity. In the meanwhile, I just called and said hello every now and then.

But one day I noticed that she never called me in return; I figured that she probably didn't accept my friendship seriously. That discouraged me, and I stopped calling her. I still liked her very much but she wasn't calling me for some reason, and whatever it was, it didn't seem to bode well for me. I was just a poor and lonesome sailor. It might not be worth it for her to commit to the friendship, and I was okay with that if that was the case.

I kept dragging forward with my condition from one dreadful day to the next; I felt especially low when I thought of my Navy career. I also realized that it was time for me tell my neurosurgeon if I wanted surgery.

I met the surgeon one day and told him I preferred not to have surgery, as the prognosis didn't seem worth the gamble. I respectfully requested to explore more physical therapy. I told him that I was willing to work very hard at physical therapy, and I hoped that might alleviate my pain so that I might return to full duty. My surgeon listened to me and sent me to more physical therapy sessions.

After six months, I hadn't spoken with the intern, and I thought she might have forgotten about this lonely sailor. I didn't regret not calling her, but I missed her. She had a nice voice over the phone that I could hardly forget.

Suddenly, she called me one evening. I was so surprised and glad to hear her voice again. She told me she had been very busy studying and she also told me good news—she had just passed the board. She was no longer an intern but a medical technologist. She had also been offered a job at the same hospital where she'd interned. I told her I was really happy for her.

It seemed like now was a good opportunity to ask her if we could meet and go out to eat. So I asked and she agreed. Wow! We had talked with each other for almost a year, and this would be the first time we'd ever met.

We met in a nice restaurant near her place. She looked so beautiful and elegant in her simple outfit. I told myself that she was the one for me. Everything went really well. I usually had constant pain, but when I saw her, I completely forgot all the pain. This happened when a young man—especially a very lonesome sailor—saw a beautiful young lady on a date. Before the lovely evening came to an end, I wanted to let her know that I was very happy to see her after we had talked with each other for so long. She also seemed very pleasant and happy. I told her that I hoped we could do this again soon. She gave me a nice smile and nodded her head.

I arrived home very late in the evening and I was very happy to have met her. I hadn't had this special feeling for a long time. She had sparked warmth in my heart. I had met her at the perfect time; I really needed a good friend. I thought that God had guided her to me so that I could survive the tough road ahead of me. I called her for the next few days, and then we met again.

Soon our meetings had become regular. We met each other two to three times a week. I thought we had become attached to each other. Although I still had pain every day, I had been very happy since I had met this beautiful girl. I believed we had special feelings for each other. I didn't feel lonely anymore.

During this time, I also heard that the Berlin Wall had completely fallen and been torn apart following President Ronald Reagan's comment three years prior. Germany was no longer divided into East and West; it had become one country with democracy and freedom. I was so happy for the East German people. They were no longer demonized by the East German Communist regime. *Why couldn't this have happened to my Vietnam fifteen years ago?* I asked myself.

It had been over three months since my new friend and I first met. One night she kissed me, and she said she loved me. Wow! That was the best feeling I'd had for so long. I told her I loved her, too. I thought God had put us together. I needed her more than ever. I prayed that we really meant for each other. If she was the one, I wanted to have our future together; I didn't want to walk the bumpy road all alone anymore.

Then a few weeks later, she told me that she wanted to start a family soon and she wanted my opinion on the matter. I thought she took the words from my mouth. All these time, I kept asking myself why my heart remained lonely; I needed a family desperately.

But I hesitated. I didn't want to say anything to her right away. I thought that we were still very new to each other and we should continue dating for a little while so we could learn and understand a little more about each other before rushing into the most crucial decision of our lives.

However, the surge of our emotion had risen very high. I soon proposed the marriage. She said yes. I was extremely happy. From now on, I was no longer the owner of a lonely heart. I would soon ask her parents' permission to marry their first daughter.

The process of obtaining permission from her parents was very difficult. They didn't seem wanting to welcome me to their family, and they didn't seem happy to grant me permission. They made me feel that I didn't deserve to marry their daughter; I was just a lonely sailor who had no establishment and no prestigious background either on my own or among my family. Then they made me go through all the difficult Vietnamese traditions for our wedding ceremony while I didn't have my own parents or family members around.

Because I loved their daughter and their daughter loved me, I ignored and overcame all the negativity from her family, and I moved on to have a wedding at last.

My wife, Duyên Thanh Húa, and I on our wedding day.

XX

$\mathscr{A}$fter our wedding, Duyên and I moved into a little apartment near my Navy base. I continued doing extensive physical therapy at the naval hospital. It seemed my symptoms improved somewhat with the therapies and medications, but some days I still had to suffer a lot. I had a wife now, though, and I was very happy. The happiness we shared seemed to dominate most of the pain I suffered. Sometimes I didn't tell her about all of my pain because I thought men don't cry. My wife knew that I had an injured back and I was undergoing treatment at the naval hospital. I told her I was very optimistic that my pain would eventually go away and that I would return to full duty; the Navy was still my ultimate career.

My doctors extended another six-month limited duty term for me, as my pain condition was getting a little better. I really appreciated that my doctors were giving me a chance to work out my problems. I focused on intensifying my physical therapy. My goal now was nothing but to become fit for full duty again.

One beautiful Sunday morning, my wife asked me to get up early so we could go to early Mass at the Saint Matthew Church in our local community. My wife wanted me to take her to the park nearby for this beautiful Sunday. We arrived and enjoyed the gorgeous weather of Jacksonville, Florida; then she told me wonderful news—she was carrying our baby. I was ecstatic, and I thanked the Lord. God knew that I needed to have a family, and he had granted me one. I had never imagined that I would have this day for myself—that I would have a family of my own.

My wife carrying our first child.

Soon, my wife gave birth to a beautiful baby girl. She had difficulty during the delivery process. The team of doctors was forced to take an alternative route to our delivery plan and perform a Cesarean section to save my baby. I was very scared at first, but the doctors told me not to worry; this had become a routine procedure. I was there to witness the whole process.

The first cry of my baby girl filled my heart and soul completely with joy and happiness. My feelings at that moment were absolutely indescribable. My wife had had surgery, but she was doing all right. I held my baby as soon as she came out of her mother's womb; then we let my baby girl rest in her mother's arm on the surgery bed. I named my first child in Vietnamese: Hồng-Uyên, which means "the love nest." I just wanted a lot of love in my own family.

My first daughter, Hồng-Uyên Hứa.

Things had been going so wonderfully. I thought I was the happiest man on earth. God had rescued me when I was almost in the pit of hopelessness. I was newly married, and now I had my first baby. I could hardly believe that I had what I had thus far. My wife and my first child were truly the most precious gifts I could receive from above. The Lord had had mercy on me and sent the gifts of love to my heart and my soul—right before I was about to fall on the road that had too many hurdles and obstacles. I couldn't thank the Lord enough.

Now every time my workday came to an end, I couldn't wait to go home and see my baby girl. Now I wasn't just a husband; I was also a father. My responsibilities grew bigger. The more I thought about my family, the more I worried. I wasn't sure about my position with the Navy, given that my back problem remained unresolved. I wished I could return to full duty today; that would have been a perfect situation for me.

One day, my chief called me into his office to tell me I would be receiving my first good conduct award for serving in the Navy for four years with good conduct. I didn't realize it had been so long; time had flown by quickly. It was good news from the Navy. Still, I anxiously awaited another piece of good news—that I would be allowed to return to full duty.

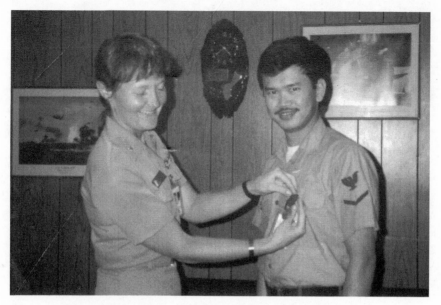

My commander awarded me the good conduct award.

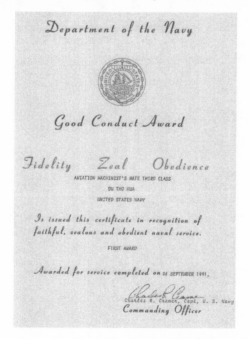

I tried to keep in touch with my other family members, especially with my mother in Vietnam. I shared with her all my good news, writing her about my marriage and telling her that she now had a brand-new granddaughter.

I missed my parents very much, particularly during special events. When my wedding took place, I was so sad that neither my mother nor my father could be there with me. I couldn't imagine how happy I would be if my parents and all of my family members had been there to share the day with me. Now a brand-new baby been born, but her grandmother was on a different continent on the other side of the earth. My father had been gone for a few years already, and now I had only my mother, so I really cared deeply for her. I wished I could live closer to her.

Meanwhile, the Communism of the Soviet Union had collapsed. What great news that was. The East German Communists had fallen and now it was time for the Communists in Russia to follow suit. The Soviet Union was the empire of the Communist world, and its regime had supported the Communists of North Vietnam in invading and defeating the South Republic of Vietnam. Now Communism no longer existed in Russia. So why did it remain in Vietnam? I didn't understand it. I wished the Vietnamese Communists would disappear from the face of the earth as soon as possible so I could see my mother in my motherland.

In addition, since I had been living in Florida, I often caught the news of the Communists of Cuba on television. I saw that the people of Cuba were also desperately trying to escape the Communist regime in hopes of reaching freedom in the United States of America. The escapees were often killed by the Cuban Communists or drowned in the ocean because their watercrafts were not seaworthy. Many times, I saw those who had made the journey get sent back to Cuba after being rescued in the high seas. I felt heartbroken for the Cuban refugees. I really wished these desperate, brave people could stay, and I totally disagreed with their being sent back. No human population should be allowed to live under a Communist party or government. I understood completely what the Cuban people had to go through. Their fates were the same as those of the people of South Vietnam.

One day, I received a letter from my sister in West Germany. She had been taking care of her family of five children, and they were doing great. They really enjoyed the freedom and democracy in Germany. All of her children were in school and some in college. I was so happy that my sister's entire family no longer lived under the Communist regime. All of her children had gotten out of Communist Vietnam in just the right time. They were young and ready to spread their wings in the sky of freedom. I knew that my nephews and nieces were ready to conquer their own destinies and futures, and I knew they were going to make their parents proud.

My sister's letter also gave me another piece of good news. The German government would allow her to sponsor our mother to come to Germany for a six-month visit, and she had already filed the paperwork. It was a brilliant idea. My brother's family in Houston, Texas, and my own family in Jacksonville, Florida, would fly to Germany, and we would see our mother, whom we hadn't seen for decades.

XXI

In the early winter of 1992, my wife and I, along with our few-months-old daughter, were getting ready for this special trip. It had been more than twenty-two years since I'd seen my mother, and I was about to see her in a country other than Vietnam. How interesting that would be and how different it was than I had imagined. It was so obvious that we never knew our fate in life. This trip would be a very long one, especially for my newborn, but I would make all the effort I could to see my own mother. I would be so happy to have my mother hold her brand-new granddaughter in her arms.

The airplane landed in Stuttgart, Germany. As we walked out the gate, I saw my mother, along with my sister and brother-in-law, standing there waiting for us. My mother immediately hugged my daughter and me in her arms, her eyes full of tears. I was so affected by seeing my mother that I was frozen, and I just couldn't say anything.

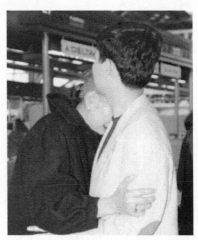

I met my mother at the airport.   *My mother hold me with tears in her eyes.*

How much I had missed spending time with my own mother. I was missing for almost a third of my life. I had always wanted to be close to my parents, to take care of them and show them the love and respect I had for them.

Although I was very fortunate and happy to meet her today, the visit was going to be so short and then we would be apart again.

I enjoyed every single moment of our time together here in Germany. I felt blessed when I saw my mother cradling my daughter in her arms. Seeing a family tie physically manifested through the generations was so wonderful. Nothing was more precious than that.

My mother with her grandchildren, holding my baby in her arms.

Time passed quickly, and our two weeks of vacation had come to an end. I felt heavyhearted as we prepared to leave my mother, not knowing when we would see each other again. Life was so tough. I remembered my mother's story of being caught in the middle of a battlefield when the Vietcong was invading the village. She had walked a long distance through the nighttime to different villages selling goods for her business, and the battle had broken out in the middle of her trip. She said missiles, grenades, and gunshots surrounded her. She jumped into a small canal and kept her head down. She thought she was going to die and that she would never return home to see her children. My mother was very lucky to be alive.

Life was really uncertain. Who knew what would happen the next day? Who knew the destinies of any existence in this universe? If we had not had to flee from the Vietcong, our big families would have lived happily in our homeland. But the evil Communists had made humankind suffer, with no regard for basic human rights and dignity. They had shamelessly brutalized and destroyed many families, breaking them into pieces. It was the Communists that made us undergo so much of the hardship in our lives.

At the airport, we prepared to fly back to the States. I wished my family could stay a much longer time. We still had an ocean of catching up and so much to do together. My soul ached deeply as I saw the tears in my mother's eyes once again. All I could say was that I loved her before my wife, my baby daughter, and I were boarding.

My mother, my eldest sister, my eldest brother, and me at the airport.

Back home in Jacksonville, Florida, it was time for me to get back to my own problems and face reality. I couldn't stop thinking about how much I wanted to return to full duty. My back injury had affected my life in every way. It had struck down most of my self-esteem and my pride in serving. I didn't like the term "limited duty" any more. I had to carry this stigma every day I went to work. I just didn't know what to do. I had worked very hard in all areas of therapy, but still no solution. I had done the recommended exercises every morning and night. I had attended every session of physical therapy. Yet the pain had never left.

I tried to forget all the negativity in my mind so I could live a normal life. I focused on my family. I felt that I was very lucky to have my wife and my beautiful daughter. When I held my daughter in my arms and fed her formula from a bottle, I looked into my baby's eyes. Many times, she smiled and enjoyed the formula at the same time. I felt so happy—I could hardly express the special feeling and precious bond of love between a father and child. It was even more precious when my baby was sleeping on my chest. I would sit in my comfy recliner and listen to her heartbeat and the rhythm of her breathing. Indeed, my daughter made me see that it was worth living another day.

One morning before we both had gotten out of bed, my wife held my hand and she surprised me with an important piece of good news. She was carrying my second child. I asked her if she was serious. I was stunned. We hadn't planned to have the second baby yet because of the situation with my career in the Navy. It was great news and I was very happy, but I was very worried at the same time. We had enjoyed great happiness with our first baby, and having a second child would be very beautiful. But a second child also meant greater responsibility.

Greater responsibility meant I needed to have a clear good future, but my future was uncertain. I believed that God had planned this for me. I shouldn't have to worry or be concerned. We all were in God's hands. I needed to rejoice in the love of our marriage and celebrate the great news of our second child. I closed my eyes and just kept holding my wife in my arms for a long time and I wished this moment would forever lasting. I loved my wife so much.

Life was getting tougher as days went on. I had my condition, and we had a small child with another one on the way. The pregnancy was very hard for my wife and I wished I could share the bearing of her physical status. I tried to help her all I could while she had morning sickness. The laughter and the cuteness of our first daughter got us through the days. We tried to tell her that she was going to have a younger brother or sister very soon, but she didn't understand yet. I was sure that she would be delighted to have a sister or brother to play with. I was so blessed with all of these bundles of joy.

It wasn't too long ago that I had been a very lonesome man. Joining and pursuing a career in the Navy in pursuit of my beliefs was my only motivation. I hadn't known I could have the family I had today. This was truly the act of God. I was so thankful for what I had received thus far. More importantly, these blessings had come at exactly the right time; I had desperately needed the love and support.

The accident that had caused my injury had become the pitfall in which I had left my confidence, self-esteem, and ability to move forward with my career in the Navy. I couldn't imagine what it would have been like to go through this by myself; the uncertainty was so great, and my Navy career was on the line. I truly appreciated the Lord so much, and I continued to pray very hard for the days to come. I prayed for my wife and the safe arrival of our new baby. I also prayed for my health to be restored and the ability to return to full duty. All of that would make me the happiest man in the universe.

My two daughters, Hồng-Uyên and Nhã-Uyên Hua.

It was the beginning of wintertime, but the sky of Jacksonville was clear and full of sunshine when my wife let me know it was time for me to take her to the hospital. I took her to the hospital and checked in. Then, following several hours of anxious waiting, we finally welcomed the arrival of our second baby girl. I was so blessed—both mother and baby were doing great. I looked at my wife; I told her I loved her. I couldn't be any happier.

I couldn't say enough how lucky and blessed I was to have my two daughters. Even though I still endured my condition, I was extremely happy and fortunate to have my two baby girls; they brought a basketful of gladness, showing me that life was precious. I loved my two daughters so much, and I enjoyed every single moment I spent with them. I didn't want to take anything for granted, and I appreciated very much all that God had given me. I took one day at a time, and I kept praying that I would soon be able to return to full duty.

XXII

$\mathcal{M}$y career with the Navy didn't follow along the path I had wanted to. One day I was undergoing a full reevaluation with my doctor. He told me I still had a lot of limitation and that I was still unfit for full duty. He also told me he had no choice but to have my case processed for separation from the Navy under medical conditions. The decision blew me away. My world had shattered, and my dreams of my Navy career were falling apart.

The final day for me in the Navy—April 30, 1993—arrived. I had been afraid this day would come, and now it had become a sad reality. As I signed the last pages of paperwork for separation from the Navy, my hand shook. I couldn't believe my life had to come to this. Holding the discharge papers in my hand, I slowly walked away from the office. Very dark clouds seemed to loom my way. Now I had become one of the disabled American veterans.

I walked to my car and got into the driver seat. I didn't want to start the engine. I leaned my head down on the steering wheel and closed my eyes as a million questions circled around my head. All of my wishes and expectations with the Navy had just been flushed away. I wanted to help fight and protect freedom in my new country for the rest of my life, and my premature termination was painful. My journey with the Navy had been tragically cut short. I had wanted to become a fighter pilot, but now that was only a dream. My Navy career had slipped out of my reach, and I didn't know what avenue I was going to take. I kept asking myself why my life was always so full of struggles.

I had believed that the only way I could help myself heal the deep wounds and lessen the misery I felt my family in Vietnam and my people suffering from the shameless brutality of the Communists was to join and stay with the United States Navy. Now, everything was gone in a flash.

Then I thought of my family. I asked myself what I could do. I was now the father of two babies, the husband and the man of the house, and I had become disabled. What could I do to support my family? I had so many tough questions, but no answers.

I arrived home early that day with a very sad face. I told my wife that today was my last day in the Navy. She knew how much the Navy meant to me, and she held me tightly, trying to comfort me. She said I shouldn't worry, that we would get through this tough time together. I thanked her for the empathy, but I was sure she didn't know how much pain mentally and physically I felt at the time.

April 30 was one of the saddest days of my life. Coincidently, this day was also one of the saddest days for the people of South Vietnam. On the same day twenty-eight years earlier, the Republic of South Vietnam had been wiped off the map. The Fall of Saigon on April 30, 1975 had allowed the vampire squads of Communists to wrap around the country and suck the lifeblood of the South Vietnamese people, destroying families in each and every village.

I was very depressed; my mind was filled with pain that night. I thought this was it. This was the end of me. The word *end* kept hovering in my consciousness. It was very late at night, and I was lying in the couch with a bottle of sleeping pills in my hand. I thought that I wanted to take all of the tablets in the bottle and put an end to my misery because I just could not tolerate the pain anymore. When I was just about to do it, the images of my two baby daughters' faces appeared clearly in my mind. I immediately stood up and threw the medicine bottle away. I said to myself that I couldn't leave my daughters.

I walked into my babies' room and they were sleeping. I kissed them on their foreheads and looked at them; I told them that I loved them so much. I then walked into my room. My wife was sleeping because she was exhausted from taking care of my two daughters. She woke up as I lay down on the bed. She looked at my face and noticed the tears in my eyes. She asked me if I was all right. I simply replied softly, *"I'm okay; I'm just in a lot of pain."* She turned her face to my side and put her arm around me.

No, I didn't want to run away. I would not escape reality and leave my children fatherless. They were all I had, and I couldn't abandon them. I loved them with all my heart and soul. I had to stand up, and I didn't matter how much pain I had. They were the reason for me to live. I was a fighter, and I had always been. I would always fight through whatever I was facing one way or another so that I could be with my children and my loving wife. It was time to keep my head up and my mind wide open so I could figure out the way.

XXIII

I dug into all the paperwork that the Navy had given me at the time of discharge. I remembered being told I needed to file the paperwork with the Veteran Administration (VA) and that the VA offered programs that would help veterans go back to school. I found the information, and I started calling different offices. I finally found myself a counselor who was in charge of my program of studies; she would help me along the way.

I was so lucky to have such a counselor. She was wonderful and understanding. She was willing to go out of her way and help motivate me in any way she could so that I might find a career outside of the Navy that would fit me. It was especially nice that she comprehended my situation thoroughly; she understood that I was a young father who had just gotten out of the US Armed Forces and had a family with two small children.

My family at the time of my
separation from the US Navy.

I was soon back in college, this time attending classes at Florida Community College at Jacksonville (FCCJ). My goal was to pursue a higher education in the field within my physical ability. The first thing I needed to do was to get an associate's in arts. Then I could step up to the university level. I knew that it was going to be tough, and the challenged would be enormous, since I didn't have a strong academic background, especially given that English was still my weakest point. But I was determined.

I had been comfortable in the Navy, helping protect our freedom, and now I was fighting for the survival of my family; through it all, I had no choice but to keep moving forward no matter how many hurdles and barriers were on the road. As usual, I did better in math, chemistry, physics, and other science subjects. When it came to English, I had a tough time, but I never stop working at it. I had to take English composition I and II, which were my hardest classes, and I was very pleased with my effort.

One day, my great English composition teacher set a competition for all of her students. It was Halloween time, and our challenge was to see who could write the scariest short story then we'd to share our stories in the front of our class. I was very nervous because I didn't have enough time to prepare but I knew I did the best that I could. After writing the short story, I stood up and shared my story with the class. At the end, after the votes had been tallied, I had won the contest. My teacher also gave me a compliment. I was so surprised and happy.

My success indicated that I could convey my message and make others understand and feel the nature of the story that I wanted to tell. This was a tiny competition in our very small classroom, but my fellow students' votes had helped me climb up to the next level in terms of my confidence and self-esteem in my college. I would never forget my great English teacher and my class.

My English composition class that strengthened my confidence.

I moved on, taking several classes every semester. I studied very hard, and I also helped my wife take care of my two beautiful daughters whenever I could.

After several semesters, I eventually completed the coursework for my degree and received a degree of Associate's of Arts. I did it well. I graduated with high honors; I was very proud of myself, and I had recovered much of the confidence that I'd lost more than a year ago, even though I was still just a poor student at the junior college.

Some of my favorite classes were in the humanity subjects. I had lived with the Communist regime for several years, so I knew what humanities were and what they were not. I participated a great deal in my humanities classroom, telling my classmates about the cruelty and inhumane actions of the Vietcong. I took part in many humanity events organized by my teacher. She noticed my good attitude and behaviors, so she nominated me for the Humanities Award. I really appreciated my teacher so much for encouraging me to keep going and never give up, although the road ahead of me might be bumpy and difficult.

Some people just get things done. Others Excel.

Excellence

FCCJ
Kent Campus Student Awards

Recognizes

Du Hua

for excellence in Humanities

on this 10th day of April, 1996

Dr. Dennis P. Gallon
Kent Campus President

During this time, I had become acquainted with several families in my neighborhood and within the city. I had more opportunities to socialize with friends, and on some weekends we got together to loosen up after a long week of work or school. Interestingly I met a friend, Chuong Tô, who had led his family to escape from Vietnam in 1989. I shared with him a little bit about my background, explaining that I had been stationed on the USS *America* aircraft carrier, the Sixth Fleet of the United States Navy, and that, in 1989, my ship had been conducting exercises in the Pacific Ocean off the Singapore coast. I told him how I had searched the ocean in vain in the hopes that my ship would rescue a Vietnamese refugee boat.

Mr. Tô told me that my aircraft carrier could had been in the same area where his escaping boat was but his boat was rescued by another US Navy warship, USS Oldendorf, at almost the same time frame. His family was among the thirty-five refugees were saved. Hearing what he said had blown me away because I knew that I was familiar with this story in *All Hands* Navy magazine a few years ago; then I told Mr. Tô that I had read the article of his rescue and I still had that article saved. I was so excited, and I told him that I must go home to find that old piece of newspaper for him to see.

When I returned with the article and I showed to Mr. Tô. Making the story even more interesting, he told me that the youngster Petty Officer Gerome Baldwin was holding in the picture was his son, Hung Tô. Wow! How interesting! The world was really so small.

Preceding page: Nguyen helps a family fill out paper work. Left: An elderly woman prepares for the trip to the Philippines. Top: Petty Officer 1st Class Joaquin Joubert joins the youngsters in an electronic game. Above: Things are looking brighter for this young refugee in the arms of Petty Officer Gerome Baldwin.

The youngster, Hùng Tô, is the son of Chương Tô, a new friend.

Mr. Tô also told me in his own words how shocked and surprised he and the people on his boat were when they heard the voice of an American sailor, Khoi Dinh Nguyen, speaking in Vietnamese from a loudspeaker to help the refugees to understand the rescue process. Mr. Tô also showed me the picture, taken by the ship during the time of rescue, of his boat. I realized this picture wasn't posted in the *All Hands* magazine.

Mr. Tô's boat, the photo taken by someone onboard the USS Oldendorf.

For a few days after I had met him, I thought about Mr. Chuong Tô's story. What a coincidence and who would've thought? Life was so unpredictable and full of surprises. I also told Mr. Tô that I was really happy for him and his family; they had successfully escaped from the hell of the Communists and found freedom in this greatest nation. Meeting Mr. Tô made me wish again that I hadn't been discharged from the Navy. I would have been with Navy ships floating in the ocean and helping to rescue more refugee boats from the unforgiving sea. I was dreaming again, and I needed to get back to my reality.

At the same time I met Mr. Tô, I also met Mr. Bao Tran. He also told me a story that illustrated the barbaric acts of the Vietcong. Mr. Bao Tran was an officer of the Airborne Special Force of the South Vietnamese Army. He was a captain until the last days of the Republic of South Vietnam. Mr. Tran was born in North Vietnam. He told me that, when the country was divided in July 20, 1954, the Northern Region belonged to the Communists and his family had been forced to move to South Vietnam so they could be far away the Vietcong. He had grown up in the south and then, following his beliefs, joined the South Vietnamese armed forces to protect the freedom and democracy of South Vietnam.

Mr. Tran was in many combats and won many deadly, large battles against the North Vietnamese Communists. He had become a decorated soldier; nevertheless, he had also witnessed the falling of many of his brothers. Three months prior to the Fall of Saigon, Mr. Tran had been badly wounded. The Vietcong's gunshots had taken off one leg from his body and shattered the other leg.

When the Communists took over the south, although the Vietcong knew that Mr. Tran was totally handicapped; however, they still forced him to go to the hard labor camp for almost three years. Once again, the Vietcong's cruelty, the regime's lack of heart for humanity, was clear.

This regime's decision created a great anger and hatred in Mr. Tran's mind for the Vietcong. He told himself that he had escaped the Communists once when the country had been divided between north and south, and now he had to try to escape the Communists once again as soon as he could find the opportunity.

In 1982, Mr. Tran successfully escaped from Communist Vietnam and settled in Jacksonville, Florida, with his family.

I admired Mr. Tran very much after hearing his incredible story. He was one of the millions of South Vietnamese people who had witnessed the horror and brutality of the regime and we were willing to die in the pursuit of living free, with dignity and democracy.

Mr. Bảo Trân, formerly with the Airborne Division of South Vietnam.

I couldn't stop dwelling on the past and the evil of Communism. I needed to get back to my own presence. Since I had completed all the required courses at the junior college, my counselor wanted to sit down with me and discuss the next important step—choosing my field of study. With my conditions, I wasn't sure what kind of occupation I should pursue. Then I thought of my own problems. I had been in pain and taking medications every day. It would be very helpful for me to understand more about my conditions and the nature of the medications I had been taking. After I had talked about this with my counselor, she suggested that I might want to pursue a pharmacy career and study medications.

I thought that was a great idea; however, I was a little hesitant. The pharmaceutical education program would be very tough, very long, and very competitive. If I chose to study pharmacy, I would spend another year taking the pre-pharmacy prerequisites. Then I would have to take the Pharmacy College Admission Test (PCAT) prior to applying to any college of pharmacy. If I got accepted, I would then spend another four years studying the pharmacy profession. I wasn't sure that I would be able to endure all of that complexity because of my condition. My counselor understood my concerns, and she asked me to think about it and get back with her next week.

I went home and discussed, in detail, the decision I needed to make with my wife. She told me she would stand behind me in whatever I chose to do. She also liked the idea of my studying medicines. I would understand more about my condition and the medications I was taking. But she also comprehended my limitations. After weighing the pros and cons with my wife, I had made my decision.

I met with my counselor again and told her what I wanted to do. I told her I had decided to choose the pharmacy major. She reminded me that the road ahead would be long and tough but I could do it. She would encourage and support me 100 percent as long as I stayed focused. She also told me that she had no doubt I would get through the program. I thanked her for all her strong support and I promised her that, once I had determined to execute a plan, I would stay focused and keep on track. I also told her that through studying pharmacy and becoming a pharmacist, I could directly help and serve a lot of people. I would understand the pain and suffering people were facing more than anybody else. My counselor agreed with me.

XXIV

$\mathcal{M}$y plan of attack was on. I started by registering for the pre-pharmacy courses, which included higher level of math, chemistry, and biology courses. These were much tougher classes than those I had taken before, but I tackled them with everything I had. In just a few semesters, I was ready to prepare for my PCAT exam.

This was tough. The exam would cover a mountain of material, and I had to study day and night.

When I thought I was ready for the PCAT, I drove to the University of Florida for the exam. The test was really hard. There were too many questions and only a little time was allotted for every subject.

I got the results a few weeks later. I hadn't done too well, and I was disappointed with my score. This told me that I hadn't studied hard enough. I needed to study much harder and retake the PCAT exam. I used the experience of taking the first test to my advantage. Now I had a better idea of what to study, how to take the test, and what to expect. I was determined to do better the second time around.

I retook the exam a few months later, and, indeed, I received a better score. I started thinking about what colleges of pharmacy I should apply to. My last crucial step was to get through this barrier of admission to a college of pharmacy. I grew nervous thinking of all the hard work I had done to get this far. What would I do if I didn't get accepted to any of the colleges? My life had been on hold, and my family was waiting for me to get our plan of survival going.

As a result of stress and anxiety, I got very ill a few times. Pharmaceutical studies was such a competitive field that I had to do very well in all areas of study. I had to maintain a high GPA in every course so I would have a better hope for the admission. I was stressed out so often because I felt that I was in a do-or-die mode—a mission for my family.

I landed in the emergency room a few times because of the nature of my problems. I couldn't sleep and totally lost my appetite for many days. I was very skinny, and I was losing weight. Every time I went to see my doctor, I was loaded with antianxiety and anti-depression medications, appetite stimulants, and heavy painkillers, and those medications sometimes made me feel even worse. Many times, I just wanted to give up and commit suicide. If I hadn't had my two beautiful daughters and my loving wife, I would have disappeared from the face of the planet. This journey was so tough—tougher than anyone could imagine. Even though I was a young father who was suffering from a condition, I nevertheless had to go through this tough road in order to ensure the survival of my family.

My life was very rough, and I was struggling; but I just had to keep going. I reminded myself that I was a fighter, so I had to fight until my last breath. I wanted to maximize my chances of getting admitted, so I applied to several colleges of pharmacy, some of which were out of state. Out of several applications, I received three responses for admission interviews. I was very excited and hopeful that one of the schools would accept me.

My first interview was with the Mercer University in Atlanta, Georgia. I had to drive the long distance by myself; my wife couldn't help me because she had to take care of the children. I had a difficult time driving, but I made it there. I had to drive to Xavier University in Louisiana for my second interview. Once again, the long drive alone killed me because of my condition. My last interview was with Nova Southeastern University in Fort Lauderdale, Florida. I thought I did well in all three interviews, and I felt the most comfortable with Nova Southeastern University. Now the waiting game began and that would last several weeks.

One afternoon when I was in my backyard planting vegetables, I heard my phone ringing. I rushed in to answer it. As soon as I picked up the phone, I heard, "*This is the college of pharmacy admission office at Nova Southeastern University. I'd like to speak to Mr. Du Hửa, please.*"

I almost couldn't hold my breath as an intense wave of anxiety rushed through me. I replied, "*Yes, you're speaking to Mr. Hửa.*"

"*Good afternoon, Mr. Hửa,*" the woman replied. "*I just wanted to let you know that you have been accepted into our college of pharmacy.*"

"*Are you serious?*" I asked, excitement filling my veins.

"*Yes!*" she replied. "*You're in. Congratulations!*"

Oh my God! I was in disbelief. I yelled to my wife, who was bathing our daughters, and shared the good news. She came out of the bathroom and jumped up and down with me to celebrate this happy moment that I would never forget.

I still couldn't believe what was happening. I was so afraid that I was not good enough for the college of pharmacy. This was a giant shift for me. I knew that God had been watching over me. I had worked so hard, and I deserved the next step. This was one of the happiest days of my life.

Life went on, and I still had a million questions in my head. The door of the college of pharmacy had just opened, and I saw the following four years of professional schooling ahead of me. Would I be able to gain the knowledge and take on the responsibilities required to become a good pharmacist? I knew it was going to be a huge challenge, both mentally and physically. Moving to be near the college was another enormous problem when I had a family with two small daughters—whether I had to move alone or with my entire family. Question after question filled my mind. I had several months to figure everything out. I could only pray and hope that everything was going to be all right.

The move was the first thing I wanted to discuss with my wife. The college was more than five hours away. I told her I didn't want to move alone and leave her and my two daughters here in Jacksonville. First, I loved my daughters, and I wanted to connect with them every day. Living more than five hours away and not seeing them every day would be punishment for me. Besides, how would my wife manage to take care of two small kids and go to work at the same time? She would need my help in everyday life to take care of our daughters. In addition, while I was going through the tough program, I would really need emotional support from my wife and children to keep me going. I didn't seem to believe I had it in me to do it alone and live far away from my loving family. I tried to explain how I felt and analyze the situation so that my wife would understand.

Unfortunately, we were just like any other ordinary couples that usually have difference in opinion. Since I loved her and I respected her ideas, I let she had her way so that she would be happy. She told me that she had a job and loved her workplace where she was. She didn't want to sell the house and move to south Florida. I had to accept her plan and moved on.

I thought it would be so painful that we had to be so far apart. I tried to talk with her again, but she had made up her mind. I had to give up my idea and do it her way. We went down to the Fort Lauderdale area to find a small place and then I made the move alone. I intended to give the effort 200 percent effort, and I hoped and prayed I could make it through the next four difficult years.

Soon, time was up and I had to move to the college alone. I would never forget the day when I said a difficult good-bye to my wife. Leaving my daughters broke my heart, even though I knew I would come back home to visit whenever I could. I pulled my car out of the driveway and moved forward. Before making the turn at the corner at the end of the road, I turned and looked at my house for the last time. Tears poured down in a way that had never happened to me before. The excruciating pain was unbearable for my heart and soul, much worse than the pain of my physical conditions. I was unable to stop the tears as my car moved farther and farther away.

XXV

$\mathscr{I}$ tried to settle down at my new place and set my mind in school. I tried to keep daily tasks like cooking, cleaning, and laundry simple. My experience in the Navy had taught me how to take care of myself. My priority was school, school, and school.

The first semester started. Oh my goodness! I had to take more than twenty credit hours for the semester. I had never done this before. From now on, I wouldn't have time to eat, sleep, or even watch news on television. The schedule would be intense. But I figured that, if anybody could do it, I could. I knew I would have to work harder than I ever had before, and that was okay for me.

Before I knew it, I had made it almost halfway through the semester, and I was doing all right. I had studied very hard. Sometimes, though, I struggled immensely. Many times, I couldn't concentrate because of the dull pain in my back and right leg. I knew that struggling was the name of the game for me, but I would never surrender.

Coming home to an empty place was also very difficult. I would sit on the couch for a long time thinking of my two beautiful daughters and missing them dearly. On many days, I was so discouraged with school that I wanted to drive back to Jacksonville to see my wife and children. I had to keep reinforcing and reminding myself. I had to get through this program and get it done so that my family could survive and I would have a way to build a future for my two beautiful daughters. All of my dreams of a career with the US Navy were shattered. So now I dreamed of the best possible future for my children. I wanted to have a good career so I could provide whatever they needed. I dreamed that my children would become the best citizens of their great country. I wanted them to be successful and productive so they could serve the people in this nation as much as I had dreamed.

I knew my children were very lucky. I had come from the darkest background—from the bowels of the Communist regime. The Communists had pushed me to the mud, destroyed my family, and made us suffer in every way, mentally and physically. My children's father had had to accept the very real possibility of death in order to trade for freedom. My children would never have to go through that. They had been born in the best possible country on this planet. I hoped they would thoroughly perceive and understand humanity so they would know and realize the tremendous opportunities they had on their hands. I had sacrificed everything for my ultimate freedom, and now I continued to sacrifice so my children would have the best possible lives and become the best possible citizens of the United States of America. I was and would always be their stepping-stones that could lead them to becoming the people I wanted them to be. I dreamed, hoped, and prayed that my children would not disappoint me.

I kept moving along, and the first semester came to an end. I was very happy that I had successfully passed all my classes. Before the next semester started, I had a few weeks break, so I drove back to Jacksonville to see my family. Being home again with my wife and children, I felt and smelled the love surrounding me.

But when I saw my wife's face, I noticed her exhaustion. Taking care of two small children, working, and caring for the household had taken a toll on her. There was no question about it; my wife was burning out and she had no energy left by the end of the day. I was afraid that, one day she might collapse. How many more days could she keep this up without the help of a family member? I felt an urgent need for us all to be under one roof.

I talked with my wife again, but she still refused to listen. I felt heartbroken because my ideas and opinions had been abandoned and my wife and I would be still separated. What she was doing was making it harder for me to stay focused on school and giving me more reasons to worry about my own family. What could be accomplished when two partners didn't work together and couldn't settle and solve the common problems? I felt my family was not in a good situation and there seemed nothing I could do about it. I was afraid that I would have to return to south Florida alone once again to get ready for my second semester.

The precious time I spent with my family came to an end abruptly. I loved and enjoyed every second I spent with my wife and daughters. I truly loved them deeply in my heart. Unfortunately, I had to leave them once again. I was leaving my family the same way I had left last time.

Without my control, tears filled my eyes throughout almost my entire trip.

Back in the south, I would face a lot of challenges through the next semester. I had been told that every semester of the first two years would be very rough, so I mentally prepared.

The second semester started and, indeed, the level of difficulty only worsened. I tried to relax and stay calm. I had to get through this semester and study wisely. A few weeks passed, and I got a call from my wife. She had been sick and not feeling well. I didn't know what to do other than to tell her to check with her doctors right away. She was too far away, and I couldn't go home yet. The semester had just started, and I had to attend many classes every day.

She checked in with her doctors and hung on for a few weeks. Then she called me again. This time was more urgent. She told me the symptoms in her stomach had worsened and her doctors said she had to have surgery. The news blew my mind away. That was it. I went to the dean of my college and explained my situation. I had to go home to take care of my wife and my family. My family, not my school, came first.

The dean totally agreed and allowed me to skip classes. I was to let the school know how the situation was after a few days so the school could try to help. I thanked the dean so much for understanding and was on my way back to Jacksonville to see my wife.

I took my wife to the hospital and checked her in for the surgery the next day. She needed to have her gallbladder taken out because it had been giving her a lot of stomach problems. The surgery went well, and she was released from the hospital a few days later.

After resting for a few weeks at home, she had recovered quite well, and she resumed her normal work schedule. She told me the symptoms had gone away. I was so glad that having the surgery was the right decision for her. However, I had perceived that returning to the college of pharmacy at this time would entail huge problems for me. I wanted to go back to my classroom and catch up for all the days that I had missed, but how could I leave my wife and my family in this condition? She shouldn't be working and taking care of my children and the household while she still needed to rest and take it easy.

She kept telling me that she was fine and asking me to return to school and do what I needed to do. I didn't think she understood the key issue that was causing a lot of problems. Her physical and mental states had been thrown off the balance, which may have been why her health went downward.

Now was the best opportunity to talk with her about cause and effect; I would present to her the facts and evidence of what we had endured through thus far. If she continued choosing not to work with me, I didn't think I would be able to go back to school. I had a big family, and I needed a full loving support from my wife. She needed to understand that thinking and responsible action all had to go together.

I gave my effort to analyze and make her understand how crucial it was for husband and wife to be on the same wavelength. I needed her as much as she needed me. I couldn't stay in school and study while I was worrying that my wife would get sick again at home. I knew that would break my heart again. This was why we needed to work this out because we only had one family and we cared so much about the love we had for each other. Furthermore, she also needed to understand my condition. The chronic problems had stayed with me at all time and discouraged me from moving forward on this tough road, along with everything else. I finally concluded that, if our family was not going to be under one roof, the process of my making it through the college of pharmacy would be broken. I tried to make this as clear as possible for my loving wife to see.

Thank God! All of my reasoning finally sank in her mind. She finally agreed with me that we all needed to move south. This was a big and long process. I loved my wife more than ever for agreeing with me. We had to sell our house before we could make the move. I realized that I needed to take the rest of the school year off so I could solve all of my problems. I wrote a letter to the deans of the college of pharmacy and explained my situation, respectfully asking permission to come back next term.

The school showed their understanding and granted me permission to come back. I was so pleased and appreciated their generosity so much.

I had to get through the big hurdle of selling the house and moving. I wanted to save some money, so I put up a sign, "For Sale by Owner," in my front yard and on some street corners. I was lucky to find a buyer several weeks later.

Now, the process of moving began. I had to sell most of my furniture to make the move easier and for the sake of my condition. A few friends came and helped me on the day we packed all of our belongings in the rented truck. It was a very painful process for me, but I had no choice. I kept loading myself up with pain medications so I could continue moving as much as I could.

XXVI

My whole family finally arrived and settled in south Florida. We moved into a tiny house, as we were here for the sole purpose of my schooling. Everything started falling into place. We found school for our two daughters, and my wife took a job at a laboratory not too far away. I also reported to my college of pharmacy and informed the dean that I was ready to get back to school. The school gave me a warm welcome back. I was so happy to be back; I could see that my hopes and dreams were still alive for my family.

Soon, the semester had started and I had reinitiated into the process of school. I was more ready than ever, and I was confident that nothing would stop me now.

All went smoothly until I was informed of some concerns about the bone on my lower mandible. A dental screen with the VA hospital revealed that I might have a cancerous tumor in that area. The news freaked me out. I was advised to see an oral surgeon. I followed the proper procedure and met the surgeon. He told me I needed to have a biopsy; it was the only way to determine what was going on with my mandible.

I became very upset. I had an incredibly busy schedule with school, and now I had to go through this. I didn't understand why so many bad things kept happening to me. I cried out so loud in my soul, *"My God! Am I suffering enough?"*

I had no option but to follow through and get a diagnosis; I knew that bone cancer was deadly and doing so might save my life. I went to the VA hospital and checked in for the biopsy procedure. The surgeon opened my mouth and went into the tissue, cut it open, and obtained a piece of bone from that area, closing it with needle and thread. I went home with antibiotics and pain killer medications.

A few days later, the doctor informed me that I had no cancerous cells.

That was great news, but it also came with bad news. My face had severely swollen and looked like a full moon. I couldn't express enough the degree of my frustration. Those surgeons had messed up my mouth. I got a severe infection even though I was taking the medication. I couldn't eat and I could barely drink for several days. I had to skip a number of days of school. In addition, I had also lost most of the sensation in the lower left area of my mouth. Those surgeons had not only caused the infection; they had also messed up the nerve roots in the area. I had suffered a great deal through all of this. The infection and the pain in my mouth eventually subsided, but I never recovered the loss of sensation and the numbness in the lower area of my mouth.

I returned to the oral surgeon's office and the surgeon told me he wanted to do a nerve wrap, which meant another surgery, to help get my sensation back.

"Thank you but no thank you," I replied forcefully.

Now I didn't just have the numbness caused by the herniated discs in my lower back pinching my nerve roots, which had spread down to my right leg; part of my face also suffered the same problem.

Despite all of these troubles, I still managed to pass all of my courses for the semester. I went through so many struggles that I came very close to hanging myself in my carport late one night. I was not allowed to die because I had a family to take care of. I loved my daughters, and I didn't want them to grow up without a daddy. I kept reminding myself that I was a fighter. I needed to persist and tackle all of my problems until my last breath without giving up.

As the semester passed, I hoped and prayed I would have no more major problems so I could see this tough program through to the end. I had learned so much from the college of pharmacy. I really liked the courses of study, including pharmacology, anatomy and physiology, therapeutics, toxicology, and pharmacy practices. I had gained and expanded so much of my knowledge, and now I understood more about my conditions and the medications I had been taking. I had made the right decision to come back to the college of pharmacy, and I had no regrets, even though I had faced the ultimate challenges that nobody could have imagined along the road.

I had been in the pharmacy school for a while already, so I thought I was ready to be exposed to and learn about the reality of the pharmacy world. After all, I was going to be a pharmacist sooner or later. The sooner I was able to use the knowledge I had gained thus far, the better I would be able to capitalize on that knowledge. Besides, I needed some financial assistance. So I took a part-time job with a retail pharmacy. The job would make my schedule even more difficult. On most weekends, instead of studying, spending time with my kids, or relaxing, I would be working at a local pharmacy.

XXVII

$\mathscr{I}$had made it through one semester after another, and the four years of professional pharmaceutical school was coming to an end. I was so excited. I couldn't wait for graduation. I was certain I would be the happiest man in the universe on that day. Although I was close to the end of the program, I still prayed for my graduation to come every night before I went to bed.

Indeed, that most important day finally arrived. Memorial weekend of 2001 was one of the biggest days of my life—my graduation. As I was putting on my graduation gown, a strange, inexplicable, special feeling welled up inside of me. I was in disbelief that I could have this day. At the time of commencement, students' names were called to come up and receive their diplomas. When my name was called, I felt the vigorous flame of happiness burning inside of me. I said to myself, *Thank you, Lord. I finally have this day.*

As soon as I had the diploma in my hand, I looked down at my loving wife and my children. I wanted to scream out from the top of my lungs, "*I did it, and I did it just for you!*" That was one of the happiest moments of my life. All of my hardest efforts and sacrifices of my wife and I had just paid off. Tears of happiness spilled from my eyes.

Shaking hand with one of the Deans.

Du Tho Hua, Pharm.D.

A great moment to have my family in my arms.

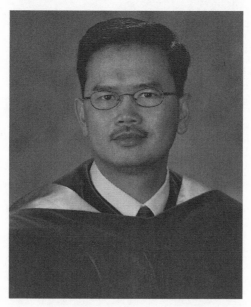

Doctor of Pharmacy, Du Tho Hua.

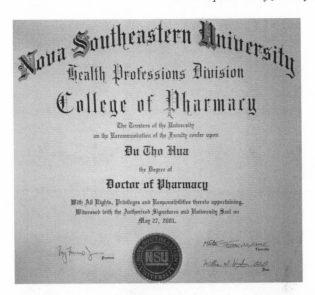

I really wanted to thank my children and my wife. My family was the whole reason that I had kept fighting for our survival. Many times I had fallen in the middle of the road, but my children had pulled me up and helped me keep going no matter how strong the storms were. The love for my children and my wife was bold, strong, and deep within my heart. My children reminded me that I shouldn't give up my weapon and shut down my brain; they gave me the courage to stand up and walk again. They were right. I listened to them and knew I should show no fear despite any barriers or pitfalls I might face.

I also needed to express my sincere gratitude to all of my counselors and the Veteran Administration. My counselors had worked very hard with the Veteran Administration to guide me on the toughest road that I had been through. My counselors were my strongest umbrellas to shelter me when I walked on the rainy streets. They had covered me through all the storms so I could continue standing up and walking. They had believed in me and given me their full support. I couldn't say enough how much love and appreciation I had for them.

I still had another small hurdle to overcome after graduation. I needed to be licensed so that I could work as a regular pharmacist. I had to pass the North American Pharmacist Licensure Examination (NAPLEX) and the Multistate Pharmacy Jurisprudence Examination (MPJE). These two exams could be very tough and costly. The pressure was still on for me. I studied extensively and intensively for several weeks. I was told that the MPJE, which was the law exam, could be very tricky and very hard to pass and that made me worry even more.

After all my thorough preparations, I was confident that I could do it. I took the two exams, and I passed them both. I was ecstatic.

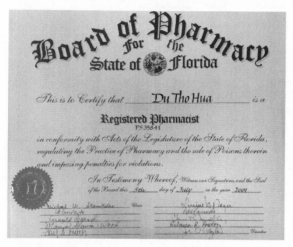

After all the wonderful news, my family was so proud of me. I felt great about my accomplishments.

But then something happened that horrified our entire universe—the event of 9/11. I would always remember that day very well. It was my day off, and I was still in bed when my wife called me from her work place. She told me that New York City had been bombed. I was still half asleep and didn't believe what my wife was trying to tell me.

"What do you mean we were bombed?" I asked.

She told me to turn on the television, and I would see for myself. I immediately turned on the TV set, and I couldn't believe what I saw. I witnessed the fire and the collapses of the twin towers after the airplanes hits them, and I thought the world had just come to an end. As I stared at the TV set, my feelings froze. No words could describe my emotion at that time. I couldn't believe I had lived until that day to see these most horrific acts that were beyond any one's imagination. Terrorists had attacked my new country that I loved and adore, the country I had served and helped protect. Today these terrorists had attacked my new land, and I felt anger deep in my heart.

The terrorists had no regard for innocent human lives, and they had committed the most evil, cold-blooded acts of humankind. They should be condemned and prosecuted by the laws of the humanity. I could clearly relate the crimes against humanity that the terrorists had just committed to those committed by the Communist regime in Vietnam. The regime had launched a surprise and sophisticated attack, the Tet Offensive, in the middle of the most celebrated Vietnamese national holidays, taking thousands of innocent lives in South of Vietnam.

Now the 9/11 attacks had broken many American hearts; these terrorists were trying to destroy the soul of this powerful and beautiful nation. But they were totally wrong about us. We would stand up stronger and the power of this country will become mightier to defend and raise the spirit of this united nation higher than ever before. I totally believed that justice would come to the barbaric, inhumane offenders of the laws of God.

I started working as a pharmacist. However, I wanted to keep my mind open and explore other options. I met a pharmacist at a job fair who spoke with me about nuclear pharmacy, a subject I found very interesting. Pharmacists in this specialty area prepared nuclear medicines for medical diagnostic purposes and special treatments for cancer patients. After he and I had talked, he invited me to his company to get a hands-on taste of this pharmaceutical specialty. I agreed to the visit, and I started working at the company after the short, hands-on training.

With my hard work and good techniques, the manager really liked me, and he was willing to send me to Purdue University to get the extensive training I would need to get a license to practice nuclear medicine.

I took that step and also got my license in nuclear pharmacy.

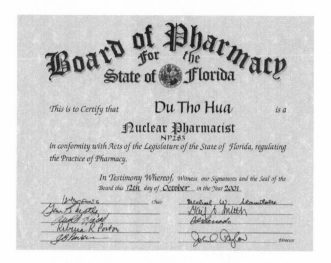

I started working in nuclear pharmacy on a regular basis. However, my condition didn't allow me to continue working there because of the bothersome schedules. I had to be at work at two o'clock in the morning; the shifts were very difficult and aggravated my condition.

I returned to retail pharmacy. I liked the retail setting much better because it gave me easy access to and the ability to help my patients. Since I had become a pharmacist, I had gained a greater sense of pride and self-esteem. In my heart, though, I still dreamed of being a Navy jet fighter pilot.

As a pharmacist, I was able to manage and work around my conditions, although I still suffered pain every day. Because of my own medical conditions, I had a lot of compassion for my patients. I always wanted to do what I could to help my people.

I had been settling down my work and career. My mind had relaxed now that I was out of school. But now I needed to work hard to pay back my financial debts and earn a good living for my family. In addition, my wife told me she wanted to have a third child before we all got any older.

Indeed, we got our wish; my wife conceived our third child. We were very happy, but we didn't think that we wanted a family of five living in this very tiny, old house. I worried about the situation and the space we didn't have.

We finally managed to move into a bigger home just in time to welcome my third child's arrival. One morning at the end of the second week of

August 2002, my wife gave birth to a baby boy. God had given me a boy this time, and I thanked God that mother and child were both well. A big smile crossed my face. I was so excited to welcome my very first son to our family.

My youngest daughter was ten years old. The gap between our kids' stages was big, and I personally didn't know how to go back to handling diapers and baby bottles all over again.

My two daughters were also extremely excited for their first baby brother. They invited some of their friends to come to the hospital to see their brother, and they stood around the baby and sang "Happy Birthday"—a scene that was both cute and funny. It was one of my happiest moments. The Lord had kept telling me that life was worth living, and I couldn't wait to hold my son in my arms.

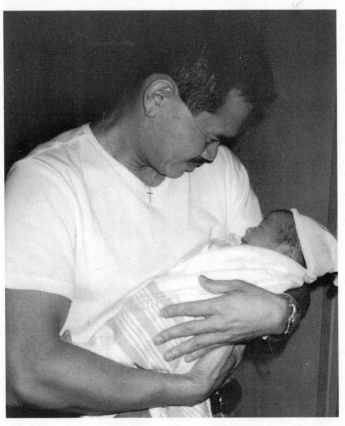

I welcome and adore my son's arrival.

Nhân-Vinh Hứa..

My three adorable children.

I continued to work very hard to take care of my family. I felt I was very lucky to have a family to look forward to at the end of my long shift, especially my new baby boy. However, some days were rough, given the nature of a big family and my conditions.

I didn't want to reveal my pain and agony I experienced at the end of the days or when I first got up early in the morning to anybody, including my wife. I didn't like complaining, and I kept my suffering to myself. I figured I was a man, a father, and a husband, and I needed to do whatever it took to take care of my family.

Sometimes I thought I should have talked and expressed a lot about the nature of my emotion and my physical conditions with my wife but I didn't. I also wanted to tell her I much I loved her ever single day for having my two beautiful daughters but I didn't say enough. I should have told her my chief complains and problems but I chose to suffer silently. I loved my children and my family so much, so I would like to focus on the main picture. I considered myself very fortunate, more so than many others. I had made my escape at last. I had found freedom in a great country. I had finally finished my school and had a job. I also had a lovely wife with adorable children. I just needed to take care of them and enjoy my family fully.

I had been working for a few years now, and the living conditions of my family had been stabilized. Being a parent taking care of my family, I thought of my own parents all the time. A different generation, environment, country, and culture would account for the evolutions and differences between the ways we raised and educated our children and the ways my parents had raised me. However, one thing that remained unchanged was respect. I had always respected my parents. I still missed them dearly. My father had been gone for a while, but I was lucky to still have my mother.

The last time I saw my mother was more than twelve years ago when she visited my sister's family in Germany. My mother was almost eighty years of age now, and I wanted to see her again.

I also knew that the relationship between the United States and Communist Vietnam had normalized. I was surprised and shocked that that could happen. The North Vietnamese Communists had started a war that had resulted in horrific wounds—especially those that had come from the evil, inhumane treatment that Communists had paid to American and the South Vietnamese. The Vietnamese Communist regime had no regard for the Geneva Agreements. I had thought these wounds could never be healed as long as the Communists still existed in my beautiful first country. The super Communist regimes of East Germany and the Soviet Union had collapsed several years ago. Why had the Communists of Vietnam not followed suit?

Life was tough and complicated, and I could find no answers to my questions. I thought of my mother at this time very much. I needed to see my mother; I might have to take a trip to Vietnam so I could see her before her health deteriorated any further.

XXVIII

$\mathcal{I}$ purchased a ticket for my trip, which I would make in the early spring of 2005. I had some concerns, as evil images of the Vietcong were always in my mind.

When my plane had landed, I walked out the gate in the old Tân Son Nhât International Airport. I saw Vietcong all over the airport, but I showed no fear. I followed the line of people, and we showed passports and documents at the main immigration checkout gates. I saw people around me put five and ten dollars bills underneath their passports or visa. I wondered and asked them why they had to do that. They told me they had to give the custom officers some money so the officers would let them go quicker, even though they had the right paperwork. If they didn't give any money, they might get retained for questioning and the officers would give them a harder time getting through the gates.

I knew it; this was how the Vietcong was. I didn't bother putting any money underneath my passport. I wanted to see what kind of hard time the officer would give me. I walked straight to the counter and handed the officer my passport without any money. He gave me a very strange look straight into my eyes, and I looked back at him, holding his gaze. He asked a few unimportant questions and I maintained eye contact and answered whatever questions he asked. Somehow, he didn't retain me but let me go.

What had just happened clearly demonstrated the corruption of the regime. I just arrived at the airport and had immediately seen these behaviors of the Vietcong. There was no doubt that corruption and decay would be apparent at every level of this ill—conceived government. They were vampires sucking the blood of the poor people in any way they could.

I continued walking out of the airport and to the main gate. I saw some of my family members there waiting for me; then I saw my mother, ready with open arms and tearful eyes. She hugged me tightly.

My mommy and me.

I was able to spend a lot of time with my mother. I took her to see our relatives. I tried all I could to make her happy and proud of a son who hadn't seen her for so long. I felt very lucky that I still had a mother to go home to. I tried to make her laugh at every dinner table, along with other members of my family. It was time to enjoy the entire family being together.

We also talked a lot. We let each other know about the misery and difficulties we had faced when we were apart. We tried to heal all the wounds as best we could.

All the people I met told me more about the nasty way the Vietcong did business. The Communist party leaders—from the lowest levels in the small villages to the regional levels and up—showed their aggressiveness and greediness. All of them were wealthy and loaded with assets of every kind, while children as young as seven years old worked or begged for food on every corner of every road and street in every village and city and on the recycled piles of trash. The Communist leaders knew sophisticated ways to make their wealth from the poorest families of their own citizens. They called themselves the heaven of Communism. They exemplified the worst within humankind.

Two weeks passed very quickly, and it was time for me to say good-bye to my mommy. Seeing her get older every day was doleful. My heart and soul were very heavy as I left her. I kept looking back and waving at my mother until I couldn't see in the distance. I cried inside, as I didn't know when I could go back and see her again or whether I would ever have another chance. I loved my mother, and the desperate thoughts sunk deep in my soul.

XXIX

*B*ack with my family in the States, I was very happy to be home again. I resumed my normal routines, going to work and taking care of my family. The long shifts of more than twelve hours at work were often put me in agony. Getting up early in the morning and going home very late in the evening was a very long day of walking, standing, bending, taking orders from doctors on telephone, checking, verifying prescriptions and counseling them about their medications and over-the-counter products for long periods of time could be tremendous amount of work. I had to use my ability to multitask to get through the day. I learned how to direct the workflow. I had to be fast and accurate. Filling prescriptions correctly was always my priority no matter what.

After all of that hard work and stress, I had no more energy left and was very exhausted by the end of the day. Walking, standing, bending, and running around my pharmacy for extended periods of time aggravated my condition and caused the most suffering.

Month after month and year after year passed, I continued to work very hard for my family. And despite of the hard work and stressful environment, some days my hard work was rewarding and joyful because I could see how much I helped my patients, my people. Many times, a patient would come back and give me good feedback and compliments; or patients would simply say, "Thank you!" That was all it took to keep a smile on my face and keep me going. Nothing satisfied me more that when I treated people with respect and I, in turn, received respect back from them. I called this the humanity.

Many times, I met many seniors who were Vietnam veterans. I always wanted to come to the front counter and greet them with utmost respect. These people had helped keep and protect peace and freedom in South Vietnam. They had sacrificed themselves, staying in the battlefields and pushing away the evil, invading North Vietnamese Communists. I wanted to shake the hands of all the Vietnam veterans; truthfully, I wanted to be their friend. I always enjoyed sitting down with them and listening to their battle stories. I would always want to tell each and every one of them, "Thank you for trying to help save the Republic of South Vietnam."

Every single Vietnam Veteran was my hero, and I appreciated all of them from the bottom of my heart for being the soldiers who had fought for my country. Now, it was an honor for me to have the opportunity to serve them as my patients. I was more than delighted, and I would go out of my way to help them as much as I could.

One day I met a very special friend who was also my patient. His name is George Lappas from Coral Springs, Florida. He got wounded in a battle and captured by the Vietcong. Despite his wound, he had shown his courage, and without the fear of the Communists, he had escaped from the Vietcong's prison but got lost in the dark jungle for two weeks. Mr. Lappas had finally got the rescue from his teammates. He had been decorated with the Purple Heart. What a story it was! He gave me his picture taken during his tour of duty in Vietnam and I was so happy when he told me that I am always his true friend. It was definitely an honor for me to know Mr. Lappas. I always wished him well and prayed for his good health.

Mr. Lappas and his teammate during their service in Vietnam.

I thought of people like Mr. Lappas all the time. He was a very well decorated soldier. I am sure he had gone through so much during his tour of duties in Vietnam. He had represented the American people, and he had shown his bravery and fearlessness to the evil Communists in trying to help secure freedom and democracy for the people of South Vietnam. Men like Mr. Lappas—along with millions of American soldiers and veterans who have been sacrificing themselves and following the quest to protect freedom and democracy, not just for America but also for the world—should be well respected.

However, when I spoke with some other Vietnam veterans, they told me many heartfelt stories. They said that when United States involvement in the war in Vietnam came to a forceful end, many soldiers who were fortunate enough to come back weren't welcomed home. I felt heartbroken and I couldn't understand that.

On March 14, 2012, I happened to watch CBS World News. I saw the American people lined up at the Dallas Airport to welcome our troops home from Afghanistan and Iraq. Among this volunteer force of welcoming troops home, there was the mailman, Mr. Randy Grizzle, who was a Vietnam veteran and he wanted to share about the feelings that his troops experienced upon their return—an experience of abandon, disregard, disrespect and deny their sacrifice.

Mr. Grizzle's had told a story of forgotten soldiers. I could see the pain and hurt inside the soul of Mr. Grizzle, who was wounded twice in battles during the Vietnam War. He explained that he has been welcoming our troops home just like he welcomed his own family members for many years, as part of his wound healing process. Mr. Grizzle is my hero. I respect him tremendously for his courage and bravery as much as all the pain and suffering he has endured.

As for all Vietnam veterans, I would really like to thank Mr. Grizzle for fighting and trying to save freedom of the Republic of South Vietnam. Likewise, in the thirty years anniversary of the Vietnam Wall Memorial, I would like to pay my utmost respect in the bottom of my heart to more than 58,000 men and women in uniform, those who fought and paid the ultimate sacrifice in an attempt to preserve freedom and democracy in Vietnam.

Here again was another example of how Communism in Vietnam had created so much pain and suffering for humanity. Their evil minds could careless about anything other than power for the Communist party. I recently happened to see a video clip about stopping Joseph Kony2012. Joseph Kony is the head of the Lord's Resistance Army, a Ugandan guerrilla group in Africa. In recent years, he has been kidnapping children and training them to become hardcore killers in Uganda. After seeing the video, I thought of the Communist of Vietnam and the children soldiers. I reflected that I went to school with many of them under the Communist regime when my family had been forced to move back to the countryside village after the Fall of Saigon in 1975. Those classmates told me many battle stories they participated when they were just very young boys. So if Kony was the worst evil of humankind, so were the Vietcong Communists, and I had no doubt about that.

Many countries still have been suffering from dictatorship of the Communism on our planet. Another prime example—Burma: The people of this country in South East Asia have been living in fear and dread of the powerful military dictatorship for decades.

But good things are coming to the people of Burma. The heroic and fearless Lady Aung San Suu Kyi has been fighting for her country for many years, and she has made successful progress, igniting change in Burma. As of this writing, the country will soon have its first free election in more than fifty years. Lady Aung San Suu Kyi will finally be allowed to run for a parliamentary seat in the government, and this very first step will symbolize the democratic reform of her country. I see a brighter tomorrow for the people of Burma, even though this is just the beginning of the change. I wish that Vietnam would also have this first step. I hope that one day I would see this become a reality for the desperate people of Vietnam.

XXX

$\mathscr{D}$uring all the years that had passed, my family had grown so much. My daughters both finished high schools and went off to college. They were no longer my babies. We had faced so many changes along the way, and I dearly missed my babies and the old times.

One thing that didn't change was my medical problems. My conditions and symptoms had been getting worse. I had been working very hard to support my family; nevertheless, I had been silently suffering so much more with my condition. Many days I would come home from a twelve-hour shift at work with excruciating pain in my lower back and my leg, and I would keep my suffering to myself without telling any members of my family. The more I withheld my pain, the more irritated and depressed I became. My worries and concerns came up even more.

I wanted to continue to support my children during their college years. But what would the future hold if my health conditions continued to go downhill? My psychiatrist had often changed and increased my antidepressant medications because of my situation. I kept asking myself how much longer I could endure my conditions. When would I reach the ending point where I said that enough was enough?

It would soon be time for me to express my feeling of pain to people surrounding me. On many days, the suffering was too much and I couldn't go to work. I stayed home and absorbed all pain physically and mentally through all of my body and soul. Sometimes I stayed home for several weeks, and I wanted to forget about working. But reality would kick in. I couldn't stay home, regardless of my aggravated conditions. I was the primary source of income for my family, and I needed to be there for my children's school and colleges.

I told myself that I had to break my silence. I wanted to let people know that I didn't want to tolerate and suffer that kind of pain anymore. But for now I had to go back to work. I had to keep biting my lips and swallowing all the unpleasant pain inside my body because I considered that there are still a lot of good strong reasons to keep me going. I am substituting the love of my family with the aggravated pain I endure every day.

Finally, I would like to acknowledge that I was so fortunate to have a great deal of support from my Veteran Affairs doctors. One of my best physicians, Doctor Kenneth Ward, treated his patients not just with the medication but also with compassion. He even thanked me for the service of my country. I couldn't tell him how much appreciation I have for him. I would also like to thank my primary physician, Doctor Sandra Romain; my psychiatrist, Doctor Mercedes Rodriguez; and my pain physician, Doctor Constantine Sarantopoulos and many other medical doctors who treated me. All of these great doctors and nurses have been helping me every step of the way. I will continue to live and be thankful for the support that I need and receive.

I also would like to especially thank my wife, who is the backbone of my support. She has encouraged me to follow my dreams in many ways. She is the love that has been easing my pain mentally and physically. I also want to thank my children for their love. I know that I wouldn't be able to make thus far without my loving family. I promise them, with God's love, that I will do whatever necessary to keep our family moving forward.

A Few Words from the Author.

My dear readers and friends,

Communism has imprinted evil images deep in my brain since I was a little boy. I have witnessed many and I can't say enough about the pernicious and horrific acts of the Vietnamese Communist regime. The people in Vietnam continue to live with and abide by the obligations of the Communist rules; because they must, they obey all the guidelines of the Communist regime. The Communist government of Vietnam continues to take the core principles of humanity away from the people of Vietnam. Absolutely no freedom of any kind exists in the beautiful country of Vietnam. Suffering and darkness continue to spread all over the sky of Vietnam. When will the suffering stop? When will justice come to the corrupt Communist leaders at every level of government? Where are freedom and democracy in this gorgeous, coastal country? When will we say enough is enough to those greedy, rapacious Vietnamese Communist leaders? The people of Vietnam continue living their daily lives without peace.

In the wake of people rising up and fighting for their freedom around the world, I feel it is imperative for all dictators and Communist leaders around the globe to learn that every human being should preserve his or her rights to have freedom and dignity. Even though my dream of serving in the US Navy was cut short and I continue to suffer as a result of my condition, I still have a different dream. My dream is that Communism will fall and cease to exist in the country of Vietnam and around the world, including those regimes in China, Cuba, and North Korea, whose government has let its own citizens starve to death so the regime could fund the building of nuclear weapons to threaten peace of the world.

We are living in the twenty-first century. As public leaders, you need to serve your own people, not suck their lifeblood to build your own fortunes. We, as the same people all over the world, shouldn't have to fight, suffer, and sacrifice for basic human rights anymore.

More recently, Communist Vietnam has demonstrated its inhumanity by arresting and throwing a young musician named Viet Khang into a hardcore Communist prison. What this poor musician did was to write two songs that stated his mind. In one of the songs, Mr. Viet Khang shared his feeling about the way the Vietcong was brutalizing and forbidding its own people from having the freedom to express. The Vietcong have taken Mr. Viet Khang away from his family and put him in a Communist jailhouse. The Vietnamese government clearly continues to commit evil acts. They have captured Mr. Viet Khang, taking him from his family simply expressing himself. Clearly, there is no freedom of expression in the Communist Vietnam.

But Mr. Viet Khang is not the only person the Vietcong has treated in this way. Many other Vietnamese people who were speaking up and expressing their feelings were also arrested and tortured in the tough jailhouse of the Vietcong.

It is time for the Communists of Vietnam to let go and free these heroes. They have done nothing wrong, and the Communists need to respect the rights of every individual human being.

The sadness continues to deepen in my heart and soul. I should have been celebrating my thirty-year anniversary of living in this great nation, but the situation in my country continues to downgrade the core values of humanity that encourage me to write this book. I need to express all my feelings about the pain and suffering the Vietcong has caused and about the fact that my people have had no choice but to endure the harshness and brutality of the Communist regime.

My dear Commanders, VFA-86 pilots, chiefs, shipmates, teammates, and friends, I would like to thank you for allowing me to include your portraits in this book. I appreciate all of your support during the times we were together fighting for the right cause. I really enjoyed all the good times and tough times when we were side by side.

I would like to welcome all of your feedback at theescapes81@gmail.com. I truly hope this book has helped you to understand more about the reality and truth of Communism.

Thank you so much from the bottom of my heart,

Du Hua.

Bibliography:

CBS World News, March 14, 2012.

Elizabeth Donovan and James Longo, As wait ends, grieving begin, Navy Times magazine, May 1989.

Jo1 Patrick E. Winter, Rescue at sea, All Hands, June 1988.

Jo1 Patrick E. Winter, Refugees rescued at sea, Transitions, August 1988.

Kony 2012. www.youtube.com/watch?v=Y4MnpzG5Sqc.

The Airwinger, Vincennes rescues 24 in South China Sea, Navy times, September 1988.

The US Navy, Rudder, Company C-014, Naval Training Center Book, 1987.

The US Navy, United States Navy Ship America (CV-66) Deployment Book, 1989.

Viet Nam Toi Dau, www.youtube.com/watch?v=9ojZ9y3pwQ8